Solar House:

A Guide for the Solar Designer

Solar House:
A Guide for the Solar Designer

Terry Galloway

AMSTERDAM • BOSTON • HEIDELBERG
• LONDON • NEW YORK • OXFORD • PARIS
• SAN DIEGO • SAN FRANCISCO
• SINGAPORE • SYDNEY • TOKYO

Architectural Press is an imprint of Elsevier

Architectural
Press

ELSEVIER

Architectural Press
An Imprint of Elsevier Limited
Linacre House, Jordan Hill, Oxford OX2 8DP
200 Wheeler Road, Burlington, MA 01803

First published 2004

British Library Cataloguing in Publication Data
A catalogue record for this book is available from the British
Library

Library of Congress Cataloguing in Publication Data
A catalog record for this book is available from the Library of
Congress

ISBN 0 7506 58312

For information on all Architectural Press publications visit
our website at www.architecturalpress.com

Typeset by Charon Tec Pvt. Ltd.
Printed and bound in Great Britain

Contents

Foreword

Octobers in the San Francisco Bay Area are always warm; and in late October, for at least a few days, the winds usually reverse direction and blow westerly, bringing even warmer air to the coastal areas from California's famous Central Valley. There is even a name for these winds: the Santa Anas. People around here inexplicably call this 'earthquake weather', but it really is fire weather. The morning of 21 October 1991, I remember noticing the balmy breeze coming from the 'wrong' direction as I left my home in the Oakland hills and drove to work. Little did I know that the East Bay landscape, along with thousands of people's lives, was about to undergo a sudden and dramatic change.

I didn't know Terry Galloway at that time. But within two days I knew the name of the street he lived on – Charing Cross. Most of the fatalities from what became known as the Oakland Firestorm occurred within one block of Terry's house, on the 14' wide, winding, steep stretch of pavement that the City of Oakland had refused to widen and which had vexed Terry and his neighbors for years. But that's another story...

It may be that if there had not been an Oakland Hills Firestorm, Terry Galloway would never have walked into my office. But I like to think that the life path we had each staked out for ourselves made our meeting inevitable. Terry had dedicated his professional life years earlier to renewable energy research and development, and had been a pioneer in promoting hydrogen fuel cells, calling for the use of medical or feedlot waste rather than petroleum to create the hydrogen. Terry had also extensively researched solar energy systems and was a strong advocate. As for me, since graduating in Mechanical Engineering from UC Berkeley in 1974, I had dedicated my life to promoting solar energy as the primary long-term energy source for the planet. So when Terry showed up at Sun Light & Power a month after the fire, I immediately knew that I had met a kindred spirit. Terry asked me to help him design and build a complete solar home, with both passive and active solar design elements. From day one Terry knew what he wanted to do with his new home, and he never wavered from his vision: he wanted his home to be a 'living laboratory'. He wanted to be able to live inside his own grand experiment in solar living. So great was his dedication that he actually lived for his first full year in the house without ever activating the back-up heating systems – because he wanted to establish a baseline performance for the passive solar systems!

Terry has always sought the latest cutting edge technologies. We discussed the pros and cons of dozens of system options, looking at radiant floor heating (not at all common in this area at the time), solar thermal water heating, pool heating and space heating, photovoltaic electricity generation (also not at all common at the time), and a ground-source heat pump as back-up (not even *heard of* around the Bay Area at the time). The hills of Oakland can get quite warm in the summer, but Terry wanted to avoid air conditioning if possible, so we crafted a night-cooling scheme that would utilize the massive concrete basement level to store 'coolth' overnight, and tied that into the ventilation system to distribute the cool air to all the rooms during the day. Terry knew this was going to be a well-insulated, tight home, so we researched heat recovery ventilation systems to bring fresh air into the house without losing valuable heat. To be sure that the house *was* built tight, we investigated the new 'SIPs' (Structural Insulated Panels), a kind of stress-skin building element using a 10" thick core of polystyrene clad with OSB board. Terry wanted his house to be 'smart', with a touch-screen computer-controlled interface that could run all of the systems and provide monitoring and data acquisition – and of course no such technology existed at the time, so we would have to invent it ourselves. We implemented all of these systems, and more. And it gives me pride to know that most of these 'new' concepts that we tried have now moved into the mainstream in the 11 years since we started building this house.

The best part was that Terry, like me, had no fear of the unknown. As pioneers and inventors, we both had great confidence in our engineering abilities. If we could conceive of it and 'prove' it to ourselves, we were willing to try it. Of course in this case this was a lot easier for me than for Terry. After all, he was the one with the open checkbook. It became a challenge for me to keep my mouth shut when I heard of, or thought of, a promising new idea, because all I had to do was mention it and Terry would say "Great, let's look into that!" and I'd be off on another research project, and by the way never mind that we were in the middle of the house construction!

Throughout the project, with an ever increasing budget, with a winter start causing us rain delays, with the City of Oakland requiring us to provide ever increasing (and unbudgeted) erosion control measures, with our structural engineer designing a $120,000 foundation system for a 2200 square foot home, with the daunting task of crafting all of the computer controls and interface for the home's multiple systems that Terry took on personally, with all that and much more, Terry was ever cheerful, ever optimistic, ever understanding, ever willing to tackle the next problem with intelligence and aplomb. Terry is a man with the rare and remarkable combinations of vision with practicality, risk-taking with meticulousness, thoughtfulness with impulsiveness – and most importantly, a kind and caring human being. He has crafted this book with as much care and thoughtfulness as he showed throughout the project. The book that he has written is rich in details and science, yet it always maintains an easy, personable nature – just like Terry. I, for one, look forward to the years ahead, hearing more about this ongoing experiment, as Terry continues to push the green edge of sustainable design.

Gary Gerber, P.E.
Berkeley, California

Preface

My interest in solar energy was prompted by the first serious energy crisis in the US around 1972–1973, which was further aggravated by a renewed crisis in 1978.

In 1971 or so, I dug by hand (shovel and bucket) most of the hole for a swimming pool and had a swimming pool contractor (Sunkist Pools) finish it and plaster it. The first solar collectors that were plastic, inexpensive and easy to purchase were for swimming pools and consisted of polypropylene black plastic. I found that an early developer of these collectors was FAFCO in Menlo Park, CA, and I called them for a discussion. I spoke to the founder Freeman A. Ford, signed a secrecy agreement, toured his manufacturing plant in its earliest days, and I was highly motivated and became a solar energy supporter ever since.

During this time frame, I had eight of these FAFCO swimming pool heating solar collectors installed on the roof of my house. One of the collectors had one of the earliest serial numbers of those produced at Menlo Park. They performed so well in heating the pool, the gas heater (required then by City code) was turned off. I wrote many technical papers about these FAFCO collectors and their performance and suggested novel ways to make use of this new technology. I had to keep these collectors swept clean of leaves and any holes created from falling tree branches had to be patched. There were also couplers that rusted, leaked and had to be replaced. But with this minor maintenance, they heated my swimming pool until October 1991, when the Berkeley firestorm destroyed my house and around 3000 other homes. I understood from FAFCO that my swimming pool system held some kind of a record of the longest continuous use of their earliest collectors.

Following the October 1991 firestorm, I had the chance to completely rebuild my early solar house using the latest solar technology. This I did making use of as many new developments in solar energy that I could find. And this book tells its readers the results of this experience.

Terry Galloway

Acknowledgements

The first acknowledgement goes to Freeman A. Ford, who introduced me to the non-glazed, polymer solar collector for heating the swimming pool. One of the FAFCO collectors was serial #00002, showing how early my love for solar began. The eight collectors heated the swimming pool to around 32°C (90°F) for each swimming season up to the Berkeley firestorm that destroyed the house in October 1991.

Next acknowledgements go to Hartford Insurance that allowed me to rebuild my early solar house using the latest solar technology and to Gary Gerber, President of Sun Light & Power as the prime and general contractor as well as Ed Nold, Architectural Designer; both of whom cheerfully undertook this huge task of bringing the most advanced ideas tempered with 15 years of solar experience. In this book you see the result of our efforts.

I also want to thank the many subcontractors that did the solar-specific installations and made them work. And, in particular, Yamas Control who upgraded my "homebrew" smart house controls to the modern world of the compact, efficient, and web-based controls used in commercial buildings today.

Finally, I thank Elsevier Architectural Press through Geoff Smaldon, who invited the effort, to Liz Whiting, Alison Yates and Jackie Holding, the dedicated typesetter team at Charon Tec, and independent reviewer Kim Sorvig for their always helpful and cheerful assistance.

List of figures

List of tables

Disclaimer

Dedication

This book is dedicated to my Great Grandfather, Daniel Best (1838–1923), who with his son Clarence Leo, co-founded the Caterpillar Tractor Company. Daniel had an incredible drive from his teen years forth to take on tough challenges and seek engineering solutions to large societal problems. He invented mechanical solutions, built them, and tested them with great satisfaction. At 21 he was one of the pioneer leaders crossing the US via the Oregon Trail, and coming up with inventive ideas along the way. Once in Oregon, he did blacksmith work, built and ran a steam logging mill, and began inventing grain cleaners and a variety of agricultural labor-saving machines. He teamed with another inventor to develop the steam traction engine to pull his newly invented combined harvesters. In 1883, this combined product was commercially manufactured in his new plant, The Best Manufacturing Co. in San Leandro, California. Steam led to vapor-electric engines, which led to diesel, and the big 8-foot traction engine drive wheels led to tracks – and so, together with his son, Daniel evolved the early, well-known and respected gas traction engine crawler tractors – the Best 30 and Best 60 models. His inventiveness continued – even at 83 he was testing new concepts in a steam turbine engine. In 1925 his son's C.L. Best Gas Traction Company and the Holt Company of Stockton, CA, merged to form the Caterpillar Tractor Company we know today.

Daniel loved sketching out mechanical designs, building them, and getting patents issued – some 38 in his name and a similar number in his son's. He loved the challenges of trying new things to encourage new technologies, leading the way to making a better world. Well, in late 2003 we demonstrated one of these huge 110 h.p. Best Traction Engines of the 1905 era, pulling a Holt Combine at the Ardenwood Historical Farm Park in Fremont, CA, harvesting 2.5 tons of wheat, culminating the result of 13 years of restoration work and thousands of hours of dozens of volunteers. This is my connection with the past, to better understand these inventive genes that drive my life today – bringing new technology forth, such as solar energy.

Goal of this guide

1.1   USERS OF THIS GUIDE BOOK

This book has been created as a Guide book to satisfy the demand of solar house designers. It is aimed to provide a unified experience base of the various solar options which designers may consider appropriate as selections, individually or in combination, for their client owner and/or architect in developing their own solar house.

The chapters have been organized into sections that cover these options and their many factors. This will help the solar designer when formulating their plans with the client/owner. Some important design guidelines that stand out as being particularly critical for the solar house designer have been highlighted.

To motivate the solar designer through this process, it is suggested that the background of the broader areas of renewable energy and the important role that solar energy plays in this mix is examined. Developing countries, many of which lack extensive infrastructure, can leapfrog ahead by skipping the problematic fossil fuel era and move into the more exciting future of new energy technologies. We also show the critical role these renewable energy options play in future global environmental health of our delicate planet and its balance of ecosystems.

The presentation begins with considerations of the construction site and how it can be used to maximize the functionality

What is renewable energy?

- solar passive heat in buildings
- solar photovoltaic (PV) power
- solar thermal power stations
- solar process heat
- solar chemistry
- wind energy
- biomass, sustainably grown
- waste-to-energy
- hydro pumped storage
- geothermal energy
- ocean energy

of the solar house, while using the direct rays of the sun to maximum advantage throughout the year. These considerations will vary tremendously depending on the part of the country in which the construction site is located.

Once these site opportunities have been carefully considered, then there are a number of solar features that can be examined, such as:

1. passive solar heat gain and cooling – siting and microclimates, and computer modeling
2. space heating from coupled greenhouse heat
3. nocturnal cooling
4. use of thermal mass for tempering the temperature swings
5. forced convection for actively controlling different zones of living space
6. radiant floor heating
7. geothermal heat pump for cooling and heating
8. domestic hot water
9. swimming pool as solar assist for heat pumps
10. swimming pool operation for 7 months out of the year
11. PV collectors for grid-tied electricity
12. computer control systems for optimizing space conditioning
13. annual energy usage
14. future.

1.2   SOLAR IS A CRITICAL PART OF THE GLOBAL RENEWABLES MIX

Global renewable energy projections

Worldwide, there seems to be a consensus within the energy-savvy scientific community that major countries should begin setting a path for renewable energy in order to provide 20% of their domestic energy by year 2020. This has far broader and bolder benefits than perhaps people realize. First, it can set their country onto a steady, dependable course to energy independence while advancing the new economy of wind, solar, and waste conversion to energy, and at the same time capitalizing on the recent advances in fuel cell technologies. Second, it can create distributed centers of energy generation with high quality, dependable, rate-stable electricity that will attract new businesses who need very reliable power.

This vision would set the individual countries of the world on a course to energy independence. By vectoring renewables on a slope upward, as shown in Figure 1.1, it sends a signal that the collective dependence on foreign oil will start its inevitable slope downward. Thus, petroleum, as the percentage of the global energy mix, will decline (Deffeyes, 2001). This message will become clear to the world around 2010. It is expected that this can release countries from the OPEC oil cartel strangle-hold currently monopolizing crude oil pricing. By 2020, renewables are expected to reach 20% of America's, as well as the world's energy mix; in fact, California has legislatively formalized this goal, and in 2002 was already at 16.5%, with wind power being the largest. The developing countries have also agreed on this 20% figure by 2020.

Natural gas and nuclear power are expected to grow slowly over the next 40 years, at which point natural gas will start its decline. It is also hoped that a new clean energy source of fusion energy will be demonstrated at increasing scales from 2030 to 2070 which will then become commercially competitive

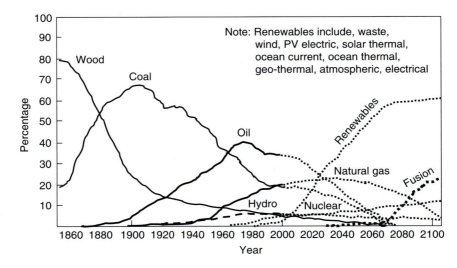

Figure 1.1   Future global energy consumption.

and will begin to pick up increasing percentages of the global energy demand into the next century.

So, it is possible that this "20% renewables by 2020" plan can set the world and the US on a stable course toward energy independence, probably starting around 2010. Now, what are the technology components of renewables? And, how do we achieve this 20% renewables contribution? Renewables around the world are defined primarily as pumped hydro-storage, wind, Geo-thermal, Municipal solid waste, wood/biomass, solar thermal, solar PVs, and other new technologies still in development. The annual growth rates of each of these technologies are shown in Figure 1.2: US Renewable Energy based on the actual commercial production/sales increases experienced from 1999 to 2000. The data points are taken from the US DOE Energy Information Agency projections for 2000 from the standpoint of an oil-dominated perspective.

Studying Figure 1.2, one can see that Municipal solid waste (MSW), Geo-thermal and Wood/biomass have all grown at 12%/year. Wind is growing annually steadily at about 30%, solar thermal heat at 26% and solar PV electric rooftop and parking lot systems at 43%. Hence, these two solar technologies are growing almost as rapidly as wind power. If all these projected growth rates for energy sources were realized, it would be

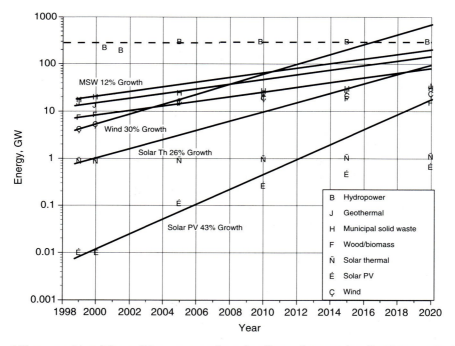

Figure 1.2   US renewables (The solid curves are from Intellergy Corporation (Intellergy, 2001) using actually achieved growth rates in 1999–2001).

possible to achieve 30% of the US energy mix or 1000 GW; however, a 20% achievement or 667 GW is a reasonable goal. We have not counted Hydropower in this summary because there has been controversy about what portion of Hydropower qualifies as renewable, as does hydro-pumped storage; thus, the Hydropower curve is shown as dashed and not added into the total renewables figure.

As shown in Figure 1.2, in the year 2020 solar thermal energy is expected to account for about 25% of the renewable energy and solar PV electricity about 2.3%. Both solar and wind energy are expected to continue at around a 25% annual growth rate in the US and around the world. Indeed, the developing countries may well be able to achieve a considerably larger growth rate of solar.

Many of these energy technologies, including solar, have a wonderful synergy with fuel cells, powered, for example, by solar PV powered electrolyzers making hydrogen or by syngas generated by steam reforming of wastes on-site. Fuel cells operating on hydrogen or hydrogen-rich syngas are very reliable, highly modular and scalable. They also provide high quality power most suitable for critical industries, such as electronics manufacturing, biotechnology, and research as well as for individual homes in the future.

1.3   ENERGY FUTURES

A great motivation for building a solar house is knowing that the solar designer is doing their part of moving our world towards a more sustainable energy future by using designs that are energy-efficient, use renewable sources of energy, and publicly exhibit the positive and very satisfying benefits, thereby helping to convince others to consider a solar house or commercial solar building.

It is clear from the section above, that the energy options humans on this earth have exploited since the 1850 coal boom, have a finite resource capacity and have clear environmental problems experienced by all of us. But one observation is quite clear: that our energy future does contain a sensible mix from which we can orchestrate a safe and secure energy future.

In this book we shall see that we can move toward renewable energy sources in our collective futures and do it in ways that will enable new vehicles of transportation, new buildings in which we can live and work, while simultaneously (albiet gradually) returning the narrow balance of our earth ecosystems back to its fundamental natural steady state.

The renewables around the world have started their steady and inexorable incline upward and we have all experienced this worldwide trend. This increase in the percentage of renewables in our portfolio of energy options has clearly begun, and we are all part of this important departure away from "business as usual." There really is a worldwide recognition of this fact by the peoples of the earth and their governments. Gradually and steadily, we, as a global people, are moving together toward renewables, of which solar energy plays a very important part.

Solar energy utilization by humans is really prehistoric – we know this by studying the habitats constructed by our ancestors who took sensible advantage of solar energy from the rays of the sun. They understood the orientation of their living areas, the storage of solar energy, and how to distribute this thermal energy to other living spaces in their habitat. Somehow we moved away from this prehistoric approach and the medieval trend in advancing solar energy emerged. We became lured by the superficial enticements of cheap fossil fuels and the ease by which they could be transported, stored, and burned. They easily released large quantities of energy to drive new life-styles and the factories and businesses on which they were so dependent. Central energy plants evolved. Now decentralized energy sources are in our future.

Solar energy technology options are much more numerous and cost-effective today than they have ever been. Solar energy is not just the passive heating of thermally massive walls or floors in an attempt to store heat into the late hours past sunset. Today, solar energy involves active technologies such as PV collectors that produce useful and economic sources of electricity which drive our electrical appliances, feed local electrical distribution micro-grids for local communities, and produce energy storage fuels (i.e. hydrogen, methanol, etc.) with the future vision of the "Hydrogen Economy" (Hoffmann, 2001; Rifkin, 2002). And what a grand vision this is indeed.

In this book, we show the solar designer how these exciting options can be achieved in carefully orchestrated steps, moving from passive solar thermal storage; active solar thermal heating; waste conversion to hydrogen; solar PV electricity generation; electrolytic production of hydrogen fuels; fuel cells; and the storage of hydrogen, each lured by the economic incentives that will become clear.

1.4   ENVIRONMENTAL PHILOSOPHY

The ecosystems of our uniquely precious planet earth are a complex equilibrium of bio-systems, easily pushed off-balance by excessive exploitation of global resources in ways that damage the environment. The environmental problems caused by extracting energy resources from the earth and the release of greenhouse gases from wasted thermal energy are two such worries. Solar energy utilization can eventually eliminate these two worries, by capturing the sun's energy and eliminating the inefficient combustion processes that produce the greenhouse gases, such as carbon dioxide.

The challenge of capturing and utilizing solar energy for electricity and heating for a house, involves the dedication of a substantial portion of the roof area for the collectors; plus the fact that solar energy is only available from 5 to 8 hours during the day when the sun is up. The new technologies available today help us overcome these challenges. In selecting these new technologies, we must understand that their production in and of themselves involves extraction and utilization of certain resources taken from the earth. Therefore, it is our responsibility to make this selection well, so that the energy needed in their manufacture, for example, does not exceed the energy these solar technologies produce. This is called "life cycle analysis." There are many solar technologies that have an excellent positive energy life cycle. We will be referring to this term throughout this book to help the solar designer make the critical selections.

1.5   NEW CONSTRUCTION OR REHAB

The installation of solar energy equipment is usually much easier and cost-effective during construction. In a new construction, it is a simple procedure to add brackets on the roof for mounting solar collectors and insert large diameter multiple conduits for carrying the power or water piping from the roof, down through the walls and into the solar equipment room. This room houses the pumps for solar heat and/or inverters that convert the DC electrical output of the PV collector to AC power to be added to the house circuits. Also in a new construction there are many ways that these collectors can be fully integrated into the roof structure itself. Building Integrated PV (BIPV) is the architect's dream for future new constructions. This involves using the BIPVs rather considerable creativity in blending the solar collectors into a building design so that they are not obtrusive.

However, with careful planning, the construction of an addition such as a solar atrium, greenhouse, porch, patio, or a garage can offer options that will allow for the cost-effective installation of solar energy in ways that may not at first been obvious. For example, on a south-facing wall, a solar atrium can be installed that will add an amazing amount of heat into a well-insulated house, doing this either passively or with a small fan. This heat can be added to the house when desired, or exhausted when it is not desired. In addition within this solar atrium, decorative and vegetable- and fruit-producing plants can be happily grown throughout the year.

Additions to a house can provide a hidden route for enclosing conduit and/or piping runs from the roof down to the solar equipment room. It is amazing how creative planning can make the installation of solar energy to a house very easy and cost-effective. Thus, this advance planning is a very important and critical part of the solar design process. The recommended steps going forward have been shown in Figure 1.3.

The logic chart depicted in Figure 1.3 shows that once the site is selected, the planning process is very much an iterative one. It is at this point, where the house is laid out on the lot, rotated on the lot to get the best solar energy performance, that different solar technologies are selected for inclusion in it, the computer energy simulation is run, and the financial payback is calculated. After any one of these steps, the results may suggest going back to an earlier step and making some adjustments. This is done iteratively, trying and exploring the possibilities. This approach should generate a number of project concepts that can be compared and discussed for considering external factors.

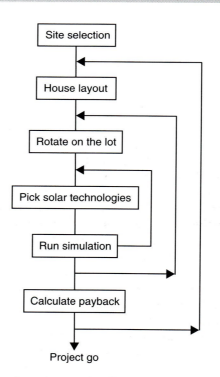

Figure 1.3   Steps for solar construction.

Once a number of preferred concepts have been developed, then the commercial computer modeling codes can be used for systems planning to explore a full variety of design issues. Some of these involve such options as roof slope and orientation, south-facing window areas, insulation, thermal mass, storage tank sizing, ground-source heat pumps, electrical and thermal load shifting, etc. Two new codes most useful for this purpose are offered by Valentin Energy Software as T*SOL and PV*SOL[1]. This would be a well-justified investment for the Solar Designer.

The financial analysis is next. This can consist of a simple payback period, which starts with the total capital cost and divides this by the annual savings from utilities costs reduced slightly by a small annual expenditure for maintenance and any consumable supplies. The result is the number of years that are required to pay back the capital investment by annual savings. If there are any rebates from various energy agencies that reduce the capital cost of purchasing solar equipment components, then these credits will be subtracted from the total capital cost. Typically these credits can amount to 25% improvements in payback time.

1.6   EXAMPLE OF THE DESIGN PROCESS

It might be helpful to give a real example of the new construction of a solar house to show how each of the steps discussed above work in practice.

Berkeley house

Starting with an empty lot, having been cleared of all debris after the Berkeley 1991 fire, the first step was to gather data on meteorology and insolation (i.e. solar flux) as well as the local microclimates, such as morning fog, summer reverse wind flow, etc. This was done, using weather records from well-known solar texts such as Duffie and Beckman, 1991, and Kreith and Kreider, 1978, as well as personal experiences from local residents. There is a wonderful new source of meteorological and solar radiation data – Meteonorm 2000, Version 4.0 (James and James, 2002), costing about €395.00 (US $395.00).

Since the lot as well as all of the surrounding land was totally bare after the fire, no shading from trees needed to be considered (generally this is the point where a site visit with a solar plotter is necessary as it will indicate where shading of the structure will occur over the range of seasons).

Next, a number of conceptual house layouts were made for the basic envelope of the structure. These were dominated by the long and large sloped roof at a 45° angle and south facing. This slope was carried from the lowest point at door height level above the outside grade up to the peak that was high enough to provide an adequate roof length for two rows of solar collectors of 8 ft length. Once this was done, the architect then began doing rough floor plan layouts to fit all the functional areas desired within the structure. At first, it was discovered that the building envelope was too small and so the decision was made to have a wing branch off the main structure at an angle to fit the lot better and provide the additional area needed. This worked well.

Figure 1.4 shows how a steeply sloped roof can be incorporated into a house design, such that the mounting of the solar collectors can be integrated into the slope and not be obtrusive. The sloped roof is important for the thermal collectors but not as important for the solar PV collectors. These points will be covered in more detail in later chapters.

Then a cardboard model was made of the building envelope. This was used to explore the location of the windows, with particular attention to those that were south facing, and the necessary summer shading to the windows from structural elements above them. The cardboard model allowed for the full exploration of solar angles throughout the seasons and minor alterations of the windows and overhang structure. This helped develop the first concept in enough detail that the computer simulation code, MicroPas 2.0, could to be used for the next step (Galloway and Miller, 1996). This code simulates all of the passive elements of the building including heat gain, heat

Figure 1.4   Sloped roof framing plan.

storage with internal thermal mass, and heat loss throughout the day by each hour, over months of seasons, for an entire year. This code quickly showed where corrections needed to be made, improvements incorporated into design features, and adjustments of windows, their area and shading. This code also had State and local agency energy requirements shown so that one could quickly tell if these were satisfied or where they were missed. Generally, solar houses are far, far superior in energy performance than those specified as minimum requirements by local or state agencies.

The following choices were made: checks were done by further iterating to see if any other improvements could be made to the system. Some examples of minor improvements needed were: (1) cooling could not be done through the radiant floor coils, since condensation occurred leading to slipping on tiles and mold in carpets, so chilled air vents were installed in each room; (2) automatic shading of the greenhouse could not be purchased and had to be abandoned; (3) the greenhouse overheated the house in summer so additional window shading had to be designed for several window banks; (4) fireplace heating required the ceiling paddles fans to operate to break up stratification; (5) the fans venting the second floor and attic heat had to be increased in capacity; (6) the noctural cooling fan bringing in cool air at night had to be increased in capacity; and (7) additional shading by planting fruit trees that provided shade in the summer and shed their leaves in the winter. Figure 1.5 shows the configuration of the completed house.

Figure 1.5   Completed Berkeley Solar house configuration.

This MicroPas 2.0 simulation was very much an iterative process. At this point adjustments were made to the building and the various solar technologies incorporated one by one to make sure they were appropriate for making the solar aspects of the building perform as desired. The use of an attached greenhouse for passive heating of the building was the most cost-effective solar feature. The floor heating was accomplished by radiant coils under the floor (tiled and carpeted areas) so that the solar thermal heat could be used effectively. Cooling was done with a ground-sourced heat pump supplying cool air via ducting to the house. An energy efficient, catalytic combustion fireplace was used for heat as the first priority during inclement weather, with the heat pump heating of radiant floor coils as back up to the fireplace. These corrections achieved the desired temperature goals and the minimum energy consumption as well as the best, optimized payback for the capital investment.

The energy controls were supplied by a commercial controls company, Yamas Controls, Inc. (www.yamas.com). Solar houses with passive and active elements require quite sophisticated controls for measuring some twenty different temperatures throughout the house, controlling eight different temperature zones, and operating some seven different heating and cooling modes. They also need to provide priority decisions between these modes, as well as exhibit the ability for the control company to dial in by phone to make improvements and maintain the system. Although not available at the time, some link to weather data predictions would be helpful to anticipate when heat storage will be needed, optimization of pool operation, etc. More of this control topic will be discussed in later Chapters.

Undoubtedly, other solar projects will differ substantially in lot location and weather types affecting heating and cooling loads for the different solar projects. I think the solar designer will find this iterative design process for solar buildings will work very well.

1.7   BUSINESS PHILOSOPHY

The design of solar houses in new construction and in remodeling is now evolving as significant new businesses around the world. These businesses have been started by technology-savvy contractors with a bent for planning and design. They also have been started by architects, who have gained substantial solar experience over the years. Whatever their background, it is important that the business founders become steeped in the knowledge of new solar technologies that have come upon the scene over the last 5 years. Inverters that convert the solar PV DC to AC power have become so cost-effective that there is no longer any incentive to specify and locate DC-powered lighting or appliances. Inverter efficiencies are now 95% to 97%, with the higher efficiency value resulting from the inverters being operated at or near their full capacity rating. Thus, connecting the inverters directly into the full house load for grid-connected houses or into the critical house loads for battery-stored remote houses, is fully desirable and cost-effective. The various worldwide manufacturers (such as Xantrex/Trace Engineering, Siemens SITOP Inverters, SMA Sunny Boy String Inverters, SunWize Technologies, Doranje Pty. Ltd, Mastervolt Solar BV, OKE, etc.) will gladly provide current data on their systems.

Another area with which the solar designer should become familiar is the fuel cell (EUREC Agency, 2002; Hoffmann, 2001). Today there are many manufacturers who will provide commercial products for houses that operate on natural gas or stored hydrogen. There is even a fuel cell store that carries a full variety of fuel cells (see www.fuelcellstore.com). This is one method for staying current on the availability of new products and their rapidly declining capital costs. There are also dedicated news services supported by the various fuel cell manufacturers that provide daily news on this topic (see www.fuelcelltoday.com).

The technology of hydrogen storage is another area of evolving new products. There are several manufacturers of dedicated hydrogen generators (i.e. Stuart Energy of Canada), based on electrolysis of tap water, who produce pressurized hydrogen in tanks such that this hydrogen can be fed directly into the tanks of hydrogen fuel cell-hybrid vehicles.

There is also the new technology of conversion of household waste into hydrogen by steam reformation for homes that are isolated from sources of natural gas. This will be discussed in later Chapters.

It will be the solar designers who study this technology who will be successful. They will be educated and experienced in these new areas, and they are most likely to form new businesses that capitalize on this worldwide, rapidly evolving, industry of solar energy.

ENDNOTE

1. Valentin Energy Software (www.valentin.de) presently in English and German. Both are wonderfully graphic and easy to use and have great technical support. There is a free demo-code that can be tried, before spending €350–520 (US $350–520) for purchase.

Site location

2.1   SOLAR INSOLATION

The energy flux from the sun falling onto a surface on the earth in watts per square meter of collector is called "insolation." The first step in examining the advantages of site location is to gather data on meteorology and insolation as well as the local microclimates, such as morning fog, summer reverse wind flow, inversions, etc. In this chapter, we will deal with the first and most important part of solar energy – insolation. This can be done, using weather records and extensive tables in the appendices from well-known solar texts, such as Duffie and Beckman (1991) and Kreith and Kreider (1978); in addition, personal visits should be made to the site with a small "solar flux meter" that measures insolation. Now there is a wonderful new source of meteorological and solar radiation data anywhere in the world, Meteonorm 2000[1] (Version 4.0).

Commonly, these insolation data, such as by Meteonorm, are integrated into commercial computer modeling codes that are used for systems planning and design. Two new codes most useful for this purpose are offered by Valentin Energy Software as T*SOL and PV*SOL[2] which would be a well-justified investment for the solar designer.

Some caution should be exercised, however, since insolation data are measured only at large nearby cities or meteorological measuring sites (such as airports), and some differences between these nearest sites and the site that is considered, can be expected. These differences occur most frequently from local fog, local clouds, and local air pollution (such as combustion particulate matter released from industrial stacks or nearby vehicular freeways). Lower insolation also arises from natural aerosols (such as terpenes from nearby local forests) and from pollution-causing (pollutants) aerosols formed by natural sub-micron particulates which photochemically grow into an urban "smog."

Near the ocean where there are marine on-shore winds, marine aerosols consisting of sea salt generated from wind-blown foam are found carrying inward the finest of these aerosols over urban areas, where they serve as nucleating agents to produce urban smog that degrades insolation.

The elevation of the site is an important factor affecting insolation at the site being considered. The higher the elevation, the clearer the sky and more free of aerosols, particulate matter, and urban smog. Generally, the photochemical smog layer is about 300 m (920 ft) on an average, and above this elevation, noticeable improvement in insolation can be observed. So when selecting potential sites for a solar home, elevation is an important consideration.

Finally, the solar designer needs to know about "air mass." Air mass is defined as the thickness of air through which the sunlight passes before striking the ground-level surface. Straight overhead (called zenith) the air mass is defined as unity and the air mass goes up directly with the secant of the angle away from the zenith. [Note: the secant is the reciprocal of the cosine.] Now, the reason the solar designer needs to know about air mass, is that thicker air mass reduces the insolation that is measured. For example, in the northern latitudes around 20°, the summer sun is nearly directly overhead at solar noon and the air mass is about 1.00. But in the winter, the sun at solar noon is not overhead and the air mass is about 1.37. So the measured solar flux will be lower by 37% below the summer solar noon value. Also the atmospheric pollutants such as aerosols, particulates, etc. adversely affect insolation more at higher air mass, since the sunlight has to pass through a thicker atmosphere (Duffie and Beckman, 1991). In another example, at a site 45° north latitude, solar noon in summer has an air mass of 1.07, while in winter solar noon has a value of 2.70.

The second factor affecting measured insolation at a site is the variation of the solar constant with calendar month. The variation of extraterrestrial solar radiation arising from the earth's elliptical orbit varies from 1322 W/m^2 on July 1 to 1413 W/m^2 on January 1. [Note: The solar radiation is, indeed, less in the northern hemisphere during the summer, and this arises from the tilt of the earth's northern hemisphere toward the sun when earth's orbit is farther from the sun. The southern hemisphere is the opposite and therefore higher in insolation.] The effect is not very large, which is about 13.8% variation from the average 1373 W/m^2 value that is accurately measured by satellites. In addition, there are minor variations of 1% or 2% arising from variations in solar activity owing to sunspots, flares, and other eruptions (Duffie and Beckman, 1991).

Consequently, a good site characterization should involve measuring the insolation at different seasons and during differing atmospheric pollution conditions. This can be done very inexpensively with a hand-held, battery-powered meter. Daystar, Inc.[3] manufactures meters of this kind. Another measuring instrument for determining insolation, and with a higher degree of certified accuracy (over wavelengths 0.3–2.8 microns) is manufactured by Kipp & Zonen (USA) Inc.,[4] which also has a data acquisition interface that permits the data to be logged on a computer.

Once the measurements are taken, they are matched with different nearby locations in the computer modeling code that have a better match to the measurements than the apparent city location that one would select. In many computer models, different site selections for summer and winter can be made to match one's local site locations better.

It is clearly worth the time spent by the solar designer examining the site and nearby polluted environs that might adversely affect the insolation, typically by $\pm 20\%$. When performing the computer modeling, energy performance calculations required for its execution and for optimal design decisions, an accuracy better than 20% will be required. [Note: The factors affecting insolation discussed above are rarely found in solar texts. So the reader now has some unique and valuable knowledge!]

2.2   WEATHER AND MICROCLIMATES

A very important initial step is to capitalize on the advantages of the site by considering solar orientation and the local weather microclimate. Seasonal site visits will help identify local wind characteristics that will control the microclimate. Orientation of the building is the most important factor in best utilizing passive solar heat gain or loss by the buildings' architectural features. These features include window areas facing south, north and to the sides, roof slope, roof or architectural overhangs providing high noon sun shading, and landscape planting with winter loss of leaves (deciduous) to capture more winter sun. A visit to the site with a solar shading indicator will reveal the impact of nearby or future trees or newly-built adjacent houses. These shading data, over a range of seasons and the local meteorological conditions, are critical inputs to any computer model that can be very effectively used to optimize house location on the site. For the author's Berkeley solar house, MicroPas4 (Version 4.50) was used. This modeling program is an excellent model that skilled energy engineers can use to help one to examine energy performance of their proposed house, interior zone by zone on an hourly basis throughout the entire year. Today other advanced state-of-the-art building energy performance models are ESP-R, TRNSYS, ENERGYPLUS and Valentin Energy Software as T*SOL and PV*SOL (www.valentin.de).

The energy engineers should visit a site and fully solar-characterize it. They can also determine critical on-site insolation levels. This is money well spent, since many options of building shape, orientation, architectural features, and landscaping can be fully explored in an interactive way in the computer model. This approach helps to eliminate the unpleasant surprises that come from spontaneous and often incorrect site planning without solar modeling homework done initially.

In the author's case, considerable optimization with the MicroPas computer simulation code was done in terms of roof slope and its azimuth orientation away from due south. The local summer microclimate in Berkeley, typically on a 3-day cycle, had thick morning fog that did not clear until late morning. This local climate was simulated by combining weather records from the more foggy Oakland airport on the west with the much warmer area of Sacramento on the east. This combination had the needed fog characteristics during night and early morning and the much warmer weather high temperatures found in the Berkeley hills in the afternoon. This modeling of the local weather revealed that more solar heat could be obtained from the roof thermal collectors if the roof was sloped more steeply (i.e. 45°) to capture more of the winter's lower sun and rotated more towards the southwest direction in order to capture more of the afternoon's fog-free sun. Once this was done, the model could also be used to optimize window overhangs for summer sun shading. This was an excellent lesson how to use the local microclimate in an energy model to optimize the design features of the solar house. Therefore, it is highly recommended that solar house homeowners, designers, and contractors make use of this very impressive computer optimization capability available today.

The example given above was for the optimization of solar thermal collectors and the solar designer may have to install solar PV collectors as well. This could be done on the same roof slope of 45°, like the Berkeley house, or they could be placed on a relatively flat roof, since the sloped condition for solar PV collectors is not as critical as for thermal collectors.

There is a fundamental difference between the two types of collectors. The thermal collectors require direct thermal rays of the sun to be optimally perpendicular to the collector to capture the maximum amount of heat. In contrast, the solar PV collectors respond to bright, white sky with maximum amount of light energy. The easiest analogy would be to guess what the PV collectors would "see" looking out at the sky over a wide angle. If they were sloped steeply at 45°, the dark ground or trees would be facing them. The PV collectors need exposure to as much bright sky as possible and the location of the solar disk is not so important. In fact, a light hazy sky or light fog can greatly (i.e. 16%) increase the PV output of these collectors over a deep blue sky that is clear. Interestingly, the reduced apparent area illuminating the PV collector with the sun more perpendicular is nearly traded off against the PV collectors seeing a larger area of bright, hazy sky.

These distinguishing characteristics between solar thermal and PV collectors will give the solar designer much more freedom and flexibility in using roof area to optimize the number and size of the solar collectors that can be installed as well as their performance to best match the site.

2.3   HEATING/COOLING NEEDS

The heating and cooling needs of a home, of course, depend on the local meteorology of the region as well as the local microclimate characteristics of the site – all of which have been discussed above.

The older, classical way of handling these needs was the concept of heating degree days and cooling degree days. These methods are found in older texts (such as Duffie and Beckman, 1991; Kreith and Kreider, 1978). Nowadays, the energy modeling codes make full use of hourly weather data archives covering the weather and insolation for different locations around the world. They usually cover 20 years, or a longer period of time to average out peculiar El Niño or La Niña conditions that have been occurring and affecting their weather to increasing severity. These weather data archives are highly recommended for use. But, as noted earlier, it should be ensured that the site or combination of two sites with the weather archives match the local site.

At this point, the designer/owner has a rough idea of a floor plan sketch, well before construction drawings. An example is shown in Figure 2.1. When the solar designer runs the computer energy modeling code, it will predict the temperatures hourly in each temperature control zone (such as, individual rooms or large common areas of the home) for every day in the year, or for selected months. It will cover a whole range of weather conditions, such as rain, light clouds, clear, etc. This fact will be easy to see when examining the model output. The insolation level will also be shown for each hour, day, month, prevailing weather type, etc. So running these simulations with weather data archives provides data for entire hypothetical year of hourly weather as one would experience living at that site. And the model will simulate how the building responds to each of these different weather types in a series, day after day. Therefore, it is actually very exciting to experience this and well worth the effort of doing detailed hourly modeling. [Note: A commercial Energy Engineer typically charges about US $500 per case run for a year's modeling.]

The variables required to supply to this modeling code are the window locations and area, the type of glass, any shading from the outside, and from the inside and how this shading changes over time during a day. The amount and location of thermal insulation usually on the outside walls or on walls next to unheated spaces, such as garages, storage rooms, etc. should be known. The amount of thermal mass, such as heavy concrete floors, thicker (double sheet rock) walls and ceilings, tiled floors, carpeting, etc. all are important input. There are other inputs also that can be provided. Table 2.1 shows the headings for a typical set of input parameters.

Some examples are necessary to understand how far-reaching and powerful this modeling could be for the performance of a home. The insulation and windows are the most important parameters and can be discussed first. There are a range of window glasses that will transmit light differently in various parts of the energy spectrum, such as in the visible and the infrared. There are also choices for using color-tinted glass. The windows could be multi-paned and additionally have a plastic film in between to greatly improve their insulating capability. The Berkeley house used triple component glass, Heat Mirror 78 on all north-facing windows and 77 for the rest. So it is important to locate windows with better insulating capability on the north side of the house where heat loss is important. On the south side a very transparent glass could be used if one needed both light and heat. However, if one needed only light and not heat radiation, a glass which transmits highly in the visible wavelengths but

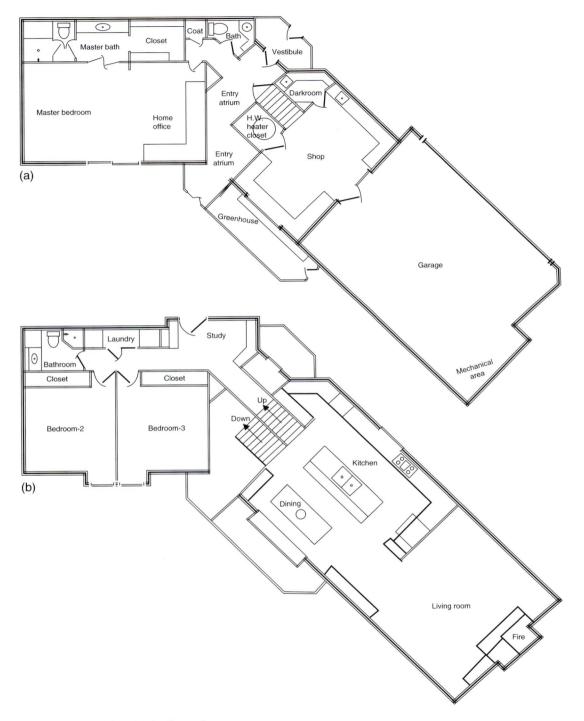

Figure 2.1 First sketch of a floor plan.

Table 2.1   Computer model input parameters.

1. Energy building code compliance requirements
    Space heating, space cooling, domestic hot water
2. General information
    Floor area, building type, building orientation, stories high
    Weather data type
    Floor construction type
    Conditioned volume, number of temperature zones
    Footprint area, slab on grade area
    Glazing percentage
    Average ceiling height
3. Building zone information
    Zone space description, floor area, volume
    Thermostat type, vent height, vent area, heated or unheated
4. Opaque surfaces
    Walls, floors, ceilings: area, insulation U- and R-value
    Surface azimuth, tilt, solar gains, shade
5. Perimeter losses
    Surface edge: length, F-value, insulation R-value, location
6. Glazing surfaces
    Window, door, skylight: area, number of panes, frame type, opening type, Azimuth, tilt, SC
    glass only, interior/exterior shade, tree shade
7. Overhangs and side fins
    Window, overhang fin: type, area, height, width, depth
8. Exterior shading
    Surface: area, screen, louver, SC of shading
9. Inter-zone surfaces
    Area, U-value, insulation R-value, location
10. Inter-zone ventilation
    Zone, vent height, vent area, location
11. Thermal mass
    Type, area, thickness, heat capacity, conductivity, surface R-value, location
12. Heating and ventilation systems
    Type, minimum efficiency, duct location, duct R-value, duct efficiency
13. Water heating systems
    Domestic hot water: capacity, insulation, R-value, efficiency, standby loss, input rating,
    pilot size, credits
14. Water heating electrical/hydronic
    Power use, operating hours, controller power, pump power

Each of these inputs can be varied as part of the design process and the modeling code run again. Since these are parametric runs of the code, the cost for studying a range of design parameters is very much less than running the code fresh from the beginning. Therefore, it is very strongly recommended that the design parametric studies be done in order to optimize the thermal and energy performance of one's home. The solar designer and the homeowner will very much enjoy this important step in the design process.

not in the infrared wavelengths could be chosen. So there is a very wide range of choices just for window glass. The modeling code allows one to make these decisions. Then the number of windows around the house is another choice. The designer

Table 2.2 Examples of thermal mass input.

Name used	Surface area (m²)	Zone	Description
Table	4.8	Living	Horizontal two sides, 38 mm thick concrete
MCSlab	32.4	Master bedroom	0.2 m covered slab in floor
AVSlab	17.3	Living	0.15 m exposed tiled covered slab
SVSlab	27.3	Shop	0.15 m exposed concrete slab
GVSlab	8.6	Solarium	0.15 m exposed brick tiled slab
MVSlab	7.0	Master bedroom	0.2 m exposed slab
Shopwall	19.8	Shop	0.2 m exposed retaining wall
MBDwall	15.4	Master bedroom	0.2 m retaining wall + 0.5″ Gyp finish
GypcrtLC	33.8	Living	38 mm (6″) covered Gypcrete in floor
GypcrtLE	30.0	Living	38 mm exposed Gypcrete in floor
GypcrtUC	46.5	Upper beds	38 mm covered Gypcrete in floor
GypcrtUE	6.3	Upper beds	38 mm exposed Gypcrete in floor
L.1.8Gyp	132.5	Living	16 mm (½″) Gypboard walls
U.1.8Gyp	69.6	Upper beds	16 mm Gypboard walls
M.1.8Gyp	68.7	Master bedroom	16 mm Gypboard walls
G.1.8Gyp	18.1	Solarium	16 mm Gypboard walls
S.1.8Gyp	28.3	Shop	16 mm Gypboard walls
S.3.4Gyp	25.4	Shop	20 mm (⅝″) Gypboard walls

has a great freedom in "tuning" the window plans to best suit the house as it will be occupied.

Table 2.2 shows a list of the thermal mass components that were used. Note, that the surface area of this mass, which is exposed to room air in motion, is the critical parameter. It is through this exposed surface that the heat is transferred by forced convection from the air moving past this surface and by conduction deep down into this thermal mass; the heat from the air being warmer than the mass is transferred into this mass and stored there. When the air temperature drops below that of the thermal mass, its heat is released outward into the room. In this way, thermal energy is stored and released when it is most needed – at nights or when air in the living space becomes cold. So in Table 2.2 the name of the thermal mass, the exposed surface area, the location, and the effective depth or thickness are tabulated. If two sides of the mass are exposed to the air than one half of the thickness is used, since heat is transferred to and from both surfaces.

With these thermal masses in addition to the building input parameters given in Table 2.2, the MicroPas4 computer model was run with the weather archive for Oakland Airport for winter time and Sacramento for summer time combined to obtain the predicted temperatures for every hour of every day, for the entire year. From the results obtained the hottest

Table 2.3   Average monthly zone temperatures throughout the Berkeley house.

Period month	Living room (°C/°F)	Master bed (°C/°F)	Upper bed (°C/°F)	Shop (°C/°F)	Solarium (°C/°F)
January	18.1/64.5	17.7/63.9	17.9/64.2	14.7/58.5	23.9/75.1
February	20.2/68.4	19.8/67.6	20.1/68.1	16.1/60.9	28.3/83.0
March	21.8/71.3	21.4/70.4	21.7/71.0	17.4/63.4	30.9/87.6
April	22.9/73.2	22.3/72.1	22.7/72.9	18.1/64.6	34.2/93.5
May	23.9/74.8	23.2/73.7	23.2/73.7	23.6/74.5	19.4/66.9
June	25.1/77.2	24.5/76.1	25.0/77.0	20.8/69.4	35.2/95.3
July	25.9/78.6	25.3/77.5	25.3/77.5	25.8/78.4	21.5/70.7
August	26.4/79.6	25.8/78.5	26.3/79.3	21.9/71.4	37.5/99.5
September	27.2/81.0	26.6/79.9	27.1/80.7	22.5/72.5	38.3/101.0
October	25.8/78.4	25.4/77.7	25.6/78.1	21.5/70.7	35.1/95.1
November	21.7/71.1	21.4/70.5	21.6/70.8	17.9/64.3	28.6/83.5
December	18.2/64.8	17.9/64.3	18.1/64.5	14.6/58.3	24.2/75.6

day giving the hottest house temperatures was August 6 and the coldest period was December 7–19.

The model predicts the average temperatures for each month of the year. These are shown in Table 2.3 as the zone temperatures throughout the Berkeley house.

It can be noted that the shop in the basement with only two small windows is the coolest and the solarium (a greenhouse) is the warmest supplying heat to the house.

Improvements that can be made with the application of movable shades during the months of May through October are shown in Table 2.4: the living room zone temperatures; then the effects of adding a shade in the solar atrium that blocks sun into the living space; and then adding shade to both the solarium as well as the solar atrium. It can be noted that the monthly average temperatures over hot summer months drop down in the living room from peaks of 27.2°C (81°F) down to 26.6°C (79.8°F) with one shade in the atrium and down to 26.1°C (78.9°F) with both shades. Of course, with shading in the solarium, its September temperature dropped from 38.3°C (101.0°F) down to 31.6°C (88.9°F).

The model showed that the hottest day in summer was August 6, where the living room temperature was at its peak of about 30.5°C (86.9°F) at 4 pm with no shades, and at 5 pm 31°C (84.8°F) with one shade, and 31°C (83.5°F) with two shades. For the master bedroom downstairs, on August 6 temperature was at its peak of about 29.3°C (83.7°F) at 5 pm with no shades, and at 5 pm 27.9°C (82.2°F) with one shade, and 27.3°C (81.2°F) with two shades.

The results of the shading study derived with the computer model suggested that the master bedroom was too hot in

Table 2.4   Average monthly living room temperatures with various solar shades.

Period month	Outside temperature (°C/°F)	With no shades (°C/°F)	With atrium shades (°C/°F)	Atrium and solarium shades (°C/°F)
January	10.2/50.4	18.2/64.5	18.1/64.5	18.2/64.5
February	11.8/53.2	20.2/68.4	20.2/68.4	20.2/68.4
March	12.6/54.6	21.8/71.3	21.8/71.3	21.8/71.3
April	13.3/55.9	22.9/73.2	22.9/73.2	22.9/73.2
May	14.6/58.3	23.8/74.8	23.7/74.6	23.6/74.5
June	16.3/61.3	25.1/77.2	24.7/76.5	24.4/75.9
July	16.9/62.4	25.9/78.6	25.2/77.3	24.7/76.4
August	16.9/62.5	26.4/79.6	25.7/78.2	25.2/77.3
September	17.8/64.0	27.2/81.0	26.6/79.8	26.1/78.9
October	16.3/61.4	25.8/78.4	25.4/77.7	25.1/77.2
November	12.8/55.1	21.7/71.1	21.7/71.0	21.7/71.0
December	10.1/50.1	18.2/64.8	18.2/64.8	18.2/64.8

summer and held its heat to 25.6°C (78.0°F) to midnight with no shades, 24.9°C (76.8°F) with one shade, and 24.4°C (75.9°F) with two shades. So further cooling of the master bedroom was achieved by installing permanent awnings over its south-facing windows which dropped the temperature to 22.2°C (72°F) which was acceptable.

Another parameter is the choice and location of thermal mass. Table 2.2 shows a list of the adjustment to the final thermal masses selected and installed. Amazingly, this is a design parameter that is generally not considered, though the role of thermal mass is a very important one. As the solar home is subjected to a full range of weather conditions covering a wide range of temperatures and wind, its interior performance is greatly improved with the appropriate use of thermal mass. For example, in a whole series of warm days followed by a very cold storm front, the thermal mass can store heat and help keep the house warm during a short period of cold weather and wind. This extra stored heat can provide additional heating of the home for a period of 3 days, reducing backup heating demand. Thermal mass can be installed in the floor, walls, ceiling and even in furniture and tiled-top tables. These new powerful modeling codes will allow the strategic placement of such thermal mass at different locations in the solar house and investigate its effect on the temperature performance and energy consumption and operating costs in both heat and cooling modes.

Table 2.5 shows the hourly temperature variations throughout the house on the hottest day of the year (August 6).

Table 2.5 Hourly temperatures on the hottest day (August 6) with shades.

Hour	Outside temperature (°C/°F)	Living area (°C/°F)	Upper bed (°C/°F)	Shop (°C/°F)	Solarium (°C/°F)	Dining table (°C/°F)
1	11.7/53.0	23.8/74.9	24.0/75.2	20.1/68.2	23.4/74.1	24.9/76.8
2	11.1/52.0	23.4/74.2	23.6/74.4	19.9/67.9	22.6/72.7	24.5/76.1
3	10.6/51.0	23.0/73.4	23.1/73.6	19.7/67.5	21.9/71.5	24.1/75.4
4	10.6/51.0	22.6/72.7	22.7/72.9	19.6/67.3	21.4/70.5	23.7/74.7
5	11.7/53.0	22.3/72.2	22.4/72.4	19.6/67.2	21.2/70.0	23.3/74.0
6	12.8/55.0	22.2/71.9	22.3/72.1	19.6/67.2	21.1/70.0	23.0/73.4
7	13.9/57.0	22.3/72.2	22.3/72.2	19.6/67.3	22.4/72.3	22.8/73.1
8	15.6/60.0	22.8/73.1	22.8/73.0	19.8/67.6	25.4/77.7	22.8/73.1
9	17.8/64.0	23.4/74.1	23.3/74.0	20.1/68.1	29.0/84.2	23.0/73.4
10	20.0/68.0	24.1/75.4	24.1/75.3	20.3/68.6	33.0/91.4	23.3/73.9
11	23.3/74.0	24.9/76.9	24.8/76.7	20.7/69.2	37.2/98.9	23.7/74.7
12	27.2/81.0	25.9/78.6	25.7/78.3	21.3/70.1	41.1/106.0	24.3/75.8
13	31.1/88.0	26.9/80.5	26.6/79.9	21.7/71.0	44.5/112.1	25.1/77.1
14	28.9/84.0	27.7/81.9	27.4/81.3	21.9/71.5	46.5/115.7	25.8/78.4
15	26.7/80.0	28.3/82.9	27.9/82.2	22.1/71.7	47.1/116.7	26.4/79.6
16	24.4/76.0	28.6/83.5	28.3/82.9	22.1/71.7	46.2/115.2	27.1/80.7
17	21.2/70.0	28.6/83.5	28.4/83.2	21.9/71.5	43.7/110.6	27.4/81.4
18	18.3/65.0	28.3/82.9	28.3/82.9	21.8/71.2	39.6/103.2	27.7/81.8
19	15.6/60.0	27.6/81.6	27.7/81.8	21.5/70.7	34.5/94.1	27.7/81.8
20	15.0/59.0	26.9/80.4	27.0/80.6	21.2/70.2	30.9/87.6	27.4/81.4
21	14.4/58.0	26.3/79.3	26.4/79.5	21.1/69.9	28.5/83.3	27.1/80.8
22	13.9/57.0	25.8/78.4	25.8/78.5	20.9/69.6	26.8/80.3	26.8/80.2
23	13.3/56.0	25.3/77.5	25.4/77.7	20.7/69.2	25.7/78.2	26.3/79.4
24	13.3/56.0	24.8/76.6	24.9/76.8	20.6/69.0	24.8/76.6	25.6/78.0

Both shades discussed above were operated to keep the temperatures down to a reasonable value. The peak temperature outside occurred at 1 pm which is 31.1°C (88.0°F). The effect this outside temperature has on the house's inside rooms can now be examined.

It is interesting to note that the temperature attained its peak inside the rooms much after the outside temperature had been at its peak. In the living room, the temperature attained its peak at 4 or 5 pm, well after the outside temperature was at its peak at 1 pm. So this is the nature of thermal mass in a house. It takes longer to rise up to that temperature and the mass holds the heat well after the outside temperature cools. In the bedrooms upstairs, the peak temperature of 28.4°C (83.2°F) occurs at 5 pm, being further delayed from heat coming from the downstairs into the upstair areas. In contrast, the basement shop reached its peak temperature of 22.1°C (71.7°F) at 3 or 4 pm.

In Table 2.5, a study of the solarium is shown, which is a glass-covered, south-facing greenhouse. Figures 2.2 (a) and (b)

(a)

Figure 2.2a,b   Photos showing solarium.

are photos of this solarium. Inside this solarium at mid height, a peak temperature of 47.1°C (116.7°F) occurs at 3 pm. As it is closely coupled to insolation, its temperature reaches its peak within few hours after the outside temperature reaches the peak at 1 pm. On the hottest day, this heat is vented out from the solarium rather than into the house, since the inside is already too hot. During winter this heat is very important in heating the house, which is discussed later.

Table 2.5 also lists the temperature of the massive dining room table, which is 550 kg (1200 lbs) of cast concrete with a

Figure 2.2a,b   Continued.

tiled top. The thermal mass in the table stores heat to help damp out the temperature swings during the day. At 1 am, the table is at 24.9°C (76.8°F) from carrying the heat from the previous hot day. The peak temperature of 27.7°C (81.8°F) occurs at 6 or 7 pm. In cold weather, carrying this heat late into the day is important.

These temperature modeling studies were done without the use of fans for nighttime cooling and without any heat pump cooling.

Now, the role of thermal mass in the passive heating of the house in the colder days of winter, December 7–19 can be examined. Table 2.6 shows a typical range of temperatures in

Table 2.6 Solar heating of the house during the cold days of winter.

December Day	Insolation		Solarium peak		Living room peak	
	kWh/m²	Btu/ft²	°C	°F	°C	°F
7	4.79	1520	49.0	120.2	22.1	71.8
8	3.38	1073	39.3	102.8	21.4	70.6
9	1.24	394	33.4	92.2	19.7	67.5
10	5.21	1654	51.2	124.1	22.8	73.1
11	4.68	1486	52.6	126.6	23.1	73.5
12	4.81	1525	50.9	123.6	22.9	73.2
13	0.16	50	24.8	76.7	18.9	66.1
14	4.35	1381	48.8	119.8	22.3	72.1
15	5.60	1777	52.7	126.8	22.8	73.0
16	5.28	1675	51.7	125.0	22.7	72.8
17	5.82	1846	53.3	128.0	22.3	72.2
18	5.69	1806	53.0	127.4	22.4	72.3
19	5.75	1823	54.2	129.6	22.4	72.3

the living room and the solarium, covering days with and without sun. The temperatures at night ranged from close to freezing to 8°C (46°F).

From Table 2.6, the insolation energy flux was normal to a surface and provided an indicator of the amount of solar energy that can be captured by the houses' sloped roof and as it passed into the solarium. Similarly there was also solar energy passing though windows into the house. It can be noted from the insolation rate that there were two storms restricting sunlight on December 9 and 13, and thus restricting the heating of the solarium during those storm periods. However, owing to the distributed thermal mass in the house, the living room air temperature lowered only to 19.7°C (67.5°F) and 18.9°C (66.1°F), otherwise the temperatures remained fairly close to 22°C (72°F). This example, thus illustrates the importance of thermal mass in stabilizing temperatures inside when there are rapid changes outside.

For those two days without sun (December 9 and 13) the house was easily heated by the heat-producing, clean fireplace (more details in Chapter 8), using three logs and clean paper refuse. With fireplace heating, the fans distributed heat only to those rooms demanding more heat. In this way, the entire house need not be heated with the fireplace, only the living room and the other rooms that required heating.

This performance was achieved entirely with passive design features. It was strongly recommended that the solar designer does everything possible and financially sensible using passive features discussed above. Only when the house was close to meeting the energy efficiency requirements of federal and/or State agencies, active mechanical components such as wood fireplace with hot air output, radiant floors, fans, and heat pumps can be considered. These features are covered in detail in Chapter 8.

A brief discussion about the heat production from the solarium is in order. The solarium must be south facing and most preferred to be below the house floor level and at grade level. This permits the extensive use of vegetables and other plants that are watered regularly on a timed drip system. The next issue about its location involves the natural circulation of air to carry its solar heat into the house. At the lowest level of the solarium, a screened door which can be opened allows the colder, lower air to be pulled in through the screen and heated in the solarium. Once heated, this lighter air can be vented into the house through a damper-controlled vent. This vent should be large enough to permit a good air circulation to remove excess heat in the solarium fast enough so that the plant temperatures do not become excessive (i.e. approximately 45°C (113°F)). The circulation of this air is driven by natural convection caused by the density difference in the air entering and leaving the solarium. It is very surprising to see how much air is actually circulated through a solarium with a conventional sliding patio door at the lower level and a $0.2\,\text{m}^2$ vent opening (12″ × 18″). Also, the higher the solarium is in design, the better the circulation. In the Berkeley house, the solarium is 1.5 stories high. Hence, the solarium concept is inexpensive; does not need fans to operate; provides substantial heating during sunny days; and adds a very pleasurable space to grow vegetable and other plants and a general visit.

The concept of nocturnal (free) cooling, affected by site location issues, is similar to the solarium, except that the cooler outside air is used. The air movement by natural convection is driven by bringing in cool air low in the building at night and exhausting the hotter air at the highest point to achieve cooling of the building. The vent opening needs to be located on the north or east side of the house where the air and surroundings are the coolest of the site. It is also helpful if the area is surrounded and shaded by plantings. The object is to pull in the coolest air as much as possible to achieve the best cooling of the house during hot summer days. The vent can be $0.2\,\text{m}^2$ (12″ × 18″) in cross sectional opening if it has no filter, but should be double this area if the incoming nocturnal cool air needs to be filtered. The hot air exhaust should be at the highest location in the building and this top vent opening should be as large as, or larger than, the lower opening. The largest possible height difference helps the natural convection process work and cool the house best.

Fans can be used to enhance this nocturnal circulation; however, they consume energy and are noisy.

2.4 PV POWER PRODUCTION

Site location issues for solar PV power production are not as critical as for passive solar heating or solar thermal collectors. The first issue is whether the site is served by an electric power company or not. The second is the location of the inverter and optionally the location for batteries. Details on the PV systems are covered in Chapter 9; thus, only the siting issues are summarized now.

PV systems can be operated in parallel with city grid power or independent. When connected to the grid, they are called "grid-tied," and these PV systems operate to supply the house needs first and put any excess power out onto the grid through the electric meter by spinning it backward, which is called "net-metering." In a cloudy weather or at night, power for the house can be drawn from the grid. No batteries are involved, since power is consumed from the utility. The optimum cost benefit is returned to the solar homeowner when the difference between the power fed to the grid and taken off the grid is very small. So that at the end of the year, after the utility calculations, the solar homeowner is charged with a smallest possible electric bill. For the Berkeley house, the typical electricity cost had been US $190 per year. About US $4 or $5 are charged monthly for taxes, fees, and other costs. With State rebates around $4.50 per peak watt capacity of the PV collectors, such solar electric systems typically have a 14-year payback or 7% return on investment. Therefore, together with possible Federal rebates and/or tax credits, the return on investment is even better.

Solar PV electric power fed onto the grid also greatly helps the utility, since it lightens the utility load especially during the hot summer days when air conditioning loads put the utilities into capacity distress. On a longer term, when there are many solar PV systems on houses and buildings, the utility must be careful that the transmission line capacity can "wheel" the power to and from the load regions that are required. The utility also has the need to insure that when the grid is down, these solar PV systems are no longer putting power onto the grid, and through the transformers producing high voltage that would injure utility lineman working on the lines. This is called "Islanding." So the inverters have design features that shutdown the inverter when there is no grid power. Newer designs being developed will allow for the continued production of power to a solar home even when the grid is down, by operating a transfer switch that removes the house from the grid so this possibly-dangerous feedback does not occur. There are many exciting future developments being explored today, and they can become commercial only when the permitting and regulatory systems have the experience and the knowledge to deal with them. So keeping the mind open to new possibilities can help local governmental agencies get current on new developments.

A variant to the solar PV application above is the concept of a local municipal solar utility or a homeowner group or a community residence association that pools their solar PV resources together. In this way, they enjoy much better economies of scale of large-scale solar PV systems that are removed from the large utility network and utilize natural gas-driven turbo-generators during power outages. There are also fuel cell systems providing electricity as well as heating for buildings in a local district. Scandinavian countries are well-experienced in such systems. The future will involve municipal and community utility systems of increasing popularity making wide use of renewable energy systems, with particular focus on solar houses.

Recently, there have been huge improvements in the cost and performance of solar PV collectors and inverters that accept the collectors' direct current power and produce 220 or 120 V AC output to be used throughout the house in all appliances, lighting, heating, and cooling systems. This has been confusing with the public, since the image of early days with direct current, low-voltage lights being required when solar PV was used. This is not necessary with the new, high-efficiency inverters. In fact, the modern solar PV inverter systems can power large heat pumps, fans, swimming pool pumps and filters, electric ovens, washers/dryers, computers, audio/video systems, etc. which could be done with the help of much better power quality than the normal grid. Computers operate very well by solar PV inverters.

The inverters are quite small now and can be placed outside or inside a garage area, near the main power distribution panel. They operate totally unattended/automatically, make only slight fan noise, and produce very little heat. Therefore, site location issues here are not critical, although location near the main distribution panel or service meter would save wiring.

ENDNOTES

1.   Meteonorm 2000, Version 4.0 (James and James, 2002), costing about €395.00 (US $395.00).

2. Valentin Energy Software (www.valentin.de) presently in English and German. Both are wonderfully graphic and easy to use and have great technical support. There is a free demo-code that can be tried, before spending €350–520 ($350–520) for purchase.
3. Daystar, Inc., 3240 Majestic Ridge, Las Cruces, NM 88011 (550) 522-4943, www.zianet.com/daystar, with a price around US $120.
4. Kipp & Zonen (USA) Inc., 125 Wilbur Place, Bohemia, NY 11716, (631) 589-2065, www.kippzonen.com, with a price of US $400 for the detector and an additional US $125 for the "Solrad Integrator" readout device.

3

Thermal mass – heated by solar and ground-coupled

3.1   AMOUNT AND DISTRIBUTION OF THERMAL MASS

The energy flux from the sun falling onto a tiled surface on the floor or a wall provides substantial heating of this surface and this heat is thermally conducted away from this surface deep down into the thermal mass and is stored for later use. This section examines the opportunities of additional heat storage by the amount and distribution of thermal mass below a tiled floor surface.

The placement of thermal mass throughout the house provides a source of heat when certain zones of the house would start to cool. Those zones which tend to cool too quickly at night or during periods of inclement weather, increased amounts of thermal mass should be placed in such zones. Generally, north-facing windows are the primary areas of heat loss since they are looking out to shaded, cooler areas of the site. So when thermal mass is placed under or near such north-facing windows, it tends to keep the space more uniform in temperature. Also when placed under the south-facing windows, such as in a window seat, the heat rising in front of the window slows down the heat loss out of the window.

There are many interesting applications of locating discretely such large thermal mass. In addition to the window applications above, the use of a very massive 500 kg (0.5 ton) dining room table, discussed in Chapter 4, which is directly illuminated by sunlight and heated during the daytime so that at nighttime eating at a warmed table is a real pleasure. This is especially true when the table is a tiled-top table, which would otherwise feel cold to touch.

Another more soothing feature is the idea of tiled floor laid over a thick concrete slab that stores heat. This can also be done in the bathrooms. Bare feet on a warm floor are more soothing than on cold-tiled floors in normal houses. The same warm floor feeling can be achieved with the concrete floor carpeted, experimented at the Berkeley house which works well, although the heat stored is comparatively lesser than the direct sunlight warming the tiles to a higher temperature. With the carpet covering, the heat conduction through the carpet and down into the concrete is slow but still significant. Thus, on a cold night, the carpet does feel noticeably warm.

Also there is an interesting application of combining the carpeted covering over the Gypcrete concrete used to encase the radiant floor-heating coils. The presence of these high-density polyethylene coils filled with glycol has little effect on the heat conduction and heat storage of the concrete slab. Any little loss with these immersed coils is more than compensated by the higher thermal conductivity of the Gypcrete used to bury these radiant heating coils. This is an excellent example of double function, where either function is not compromised by their dual function.

The best use of thermal mass is when there is sunlight falling on the surface of this mass. A tiled floor is exposed to a wide range of hours of sunlight from south-facing windows as the sunlight path moves across the floor. This is one reason tiled floors laid on a thick concrete floor slab perform so well, since they receive sunlight heating over a very large surface area and then they re-radiate at night to provide a significant source of heat.

3.2   THERMAL ENERGY STORAGE

In Chapter 2, the importance of thermal mass affecting the heating and cooling of the house had been discussed and illustrated; and also how this thermal mass can store heat during the day as the temperature of the air increases and then at night releasing the stored heat into the surrounding air to help keep the house warm. Tiled floors provide an additional opportunity for the storage of heat which can be further enhanced by the direct illumination of sunlight directly onto this tile surface.

The mechanism of conduction of heat from a tiled surface deep into the concrete slab below needs to be explained first. In addition to the advantage of dark, radiant heat-absorbing colors, the non-glossy, reflective surfaces of these tiles are very efficient absorbers of solar radiation falling onto their surface. The best way to select tiles is by collecting samples of different tiles from a local tile store and putting them out on the floor under direct sunlight passing through the window. It can be noted that the passage of sunlight through the glass slightly alters the wavelengths and the energy available to heat the tile. So doing this test inside the house is more realistic of what one would expect inside their solar house.

The tiles should be arranged on surfaces that do not need any special thermal properties, to discover how quickly these tiles warm up from the solar energy falling on their surface. After approximately an hour the temperature differences are such that the tiles are so hot to touch and they almost burn one's fingers. For additional precision, as shown in Figure 3.1, a thermometer is placed on the tile surface with a small piece of cotton or light cloth to insulate the thermometer tip from loosing heat to the outside air. The flatter the bulb down on the surface, the more accurate the temperature measurement. [Note: This can be a fascinating science fair experiment for middle school and/or high school kids.] The best tiles for a solar house are those that attain the highest temperatures. However, they are not too hot for bare feet to walk on them, since they are bonded to the concrete floor with grout or conductive adhesives that evens the temperature.

The tile is selected based on its ability to receive solar energy through the direct rays of the sun falling on them. Now this tile is affixed onto the concrete floor surface by thermally conductive grout or adhesive. By thermally conductive, it is meant that the materials should be inorganic or very dense organic adhesive that is thin and able to conduct thermal heat through the thin layer with little thermal resistance.

With the solar-absorbing tile affixed to the concrete floor, the next design choice is the type and thickness of the concrete slab. Normal concrete is the best, but light-weight concrete, used for embedding radiant floor tubing also works well since it is a special mix of highly thermal conductive materials to help the radiant floor tubes conduct the heat into the room.

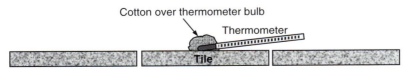

Figure 3.1   Thermometer method of selecting superior tiles for solar floor.

So, the thickness of the concrete slab is an important design parameter. The thicker the slab, the more heat stored and the longer it will release this heat into the colder night air above the floor. However, there is an optimum limit to the thickness because of the cost of the concrete and its ability to conduct heat deep into this mass at reasonably high temperatures. Generally 100–150 mm (4"–6") works well.

In Figure 3.2, the solar heating of the tiled floor over one sunny day is shown and the penetration of the solar heat down into the concrete slab below. Also the next early morning with no solar input and the slow release of the stored heat from the slab is plotted in the figure. The thermal measurements were made on the 150 mm (6") thick concrete heat storage slabs, using a pair of thermistors (10 kΩ) inserted into 10 mm (3"/8") long ID copper tubes inserted into the wet concrete from the edge at two depths, 50 and 100 mm (2" and 4"). These tubes were inserted parallel to the surface for a long distance to avoid any influence of the copper tube cooling the thermistors from the tubes' exposed end at the edge of the slab, into which the thermistor and its leads were inserted. The air temperature just above the floor was also measured and plotted in this figure. The solar flux measured by a Kipp & Zonen pyranometer (Model CM3-L) is also shown in this figure.

The temperature curves at two depths, 50 and 100 mm (2" and 4") down into the concrete can be studied. As the solar flux begins to heat the concrete the thermal wave moves down into the concrete and starts to heat the layer at 50 mm. The

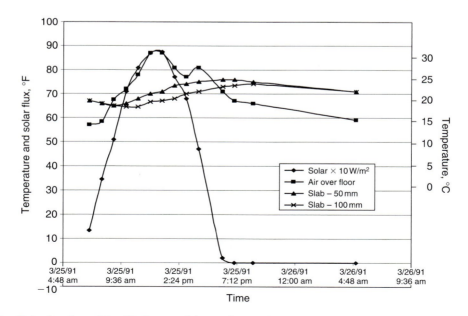

Figure 3.2   Solar heating of the tile floor and thermal mass heat storage.

noon peak of the solar flux was 880 W/m² on March 25. There was a corresponding temperature gradient down into the concrete slab at a rate of 0.05°C/mm (30°F/ft). Approximately 3 hours later, the wave reached down to the 100 mm depth. Since the concrete is 150 mm thick, the thermal wave does not reach the deepest point as the surface of the concrete starts to cool after sunset. Hence, the concrete slab need not be more than 150 mm thick to accomplish the majority of its heat storage advantage. The computer simulation codes, like Micropas4, handles this transient heat conduction in charging the slab and releasing its heat very well resulting in excellent predictions of room temperatures over different seasons of the year.

Provisions for the thermal mass in the solarium to hold the captured heat as much as possible for the release into the house after sunset had been made. The solarium is used also as a greenhouse for vegetables and other plants which shall be discussed in Chapter 4. So for early germination of seeds, the soil should be warmed for extended periods of time. This was accomplished through the use of large raised beds of 0.3 m (12″) thick soil beds exposed on all sides for absorbing heat from both the sun and warm air. This massive quantity of soil was very effective in carrying the heat well into late evening till 11 pm. The computer-controlled heating, ventilation, and air conditioning (HVAC) system held open the proper air vents allowing the cooler house air to be carried into the solarium, heated by thermal mass and then discharged through the top vent of the solarium back into the house for prolonged space heating in the evening.

Besides the use of solid materials such as tiles, concrete slabs, concrete cast tables, and radiant floor, heat can also be stored by water in tanks or drums. Piping was installed between the solarium and the garage so that water heated in the solarium could be pumped into tanks or drums in the garage so that this heat could be used for further heating of the house in areas not accessible by the warm air discharged by the air vents. However, this water should be treated with some inhibitor such as dilute glycol additive to prevent algal growth or other contamination.

With creative imagination, a wide variety of uses of thermal mass in a solar house can be promoted for further storage and distribution of heating in the solar house.

3.3 RE-RADIATION AND RELEASE OF HEAT AT NIGHT OR IN CLOUDY WEATHER

Now, the effectiveness of the thermal mass, such as a concrete slab, in re-radiating its stored heat and releasing it into the living space can be examined.

From Figure 3.2, the data shows that the slab picks up heat to reach 25°C (76°F) at 5 pm when the air temperature begins to drop below the concrete temperature. At this point the heat stored in the slab is transferred to the living space. By 4:30 am the next day, the outside air temperature had dropped to 10°C (50.1°F), compared to the air temperature just above the concrete of 15°C (60°F). This temperature driving force of 5°C (10°F) releases heat into the surrounding air at a heat transfer coefficient of 11 W/m^2-°C (2 Btu/hr-ft^2-°F). For this heating of the air on a cloudy day the next day, the concrete temperature cooled down slowly and was a very effective source of stored heat.

These kinds of thermal measurements are very useful and can provide important input for the computer thermal performance simulation programs. Pairs of temperature sensors placed just below a thermal storage floor slab to be used as standard instrumentation are also suggested for future passive designs. This will permit a large database to be developed, covering a large range of architectural geometries for this important solar heat storage component – solar heated-tiled floors.

Although not incorporated in the Berkeley solar house, the house design could include the advantage of a heavy vertical wall, called a Trombe wall, where the direct solar energy is allowed to fall onto the surface of this wall. During nighttime the opposite surface of this wall re-radiates this energy back into the living space particularly on the occupants, who can feel the warmth of this radiant heat from the wall. Although this concept is a little harder to incorporate into the design of a solar house, since the wall blocks a view out of the window that is admitting the sunlight to heat this wall, with design innovations there could be useful applications. However, the use of tiled floor or a tiled table mass was the more optimum use of interior space.

3.4   THERMAL MASS – HEATED/COOLED BY GROUND-COUPLING

Ground-coupled thermal mass is another concept that is effectively used in association with solar heated tile floors. Outstanding temperature control can be achieved by properly balancing these cooling and heating modes.

[Note: The data for this section was difficult to obtain, since they had to be taken with only the ground-coupled thermal mass controlling the temperature of a room, which was not occupied for three seasons of weather cycle.]

Figure 3.3 shows master bedroom temperature record through three seasons, unoccupied. The outdoor temperature

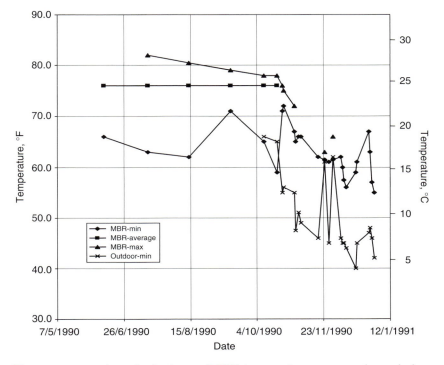

Figure 3.3   Three seasons of master bedroom (MBR) temperatures – ground-coupled.

was measured in a sheltered and shaded location on the north side of the house. The results showed that for the hottest day (August 20) with a maximum outdoor temperature of 38°C (101°F), Micropas predicted a maximum inside temperature of 25.5°C (78°F); while measurements showed 27.8°C (82°F). The figure also shows the effect of nocturnal cooling that brought cool night time air into the master bedroom upward through the house and exited at the second story roofline, thus achieving a consistent minimum temperature of 16.7°C (62°F) inside at nights during the July–August summer months. Nocturnal cooling will be discussed in detail in Chapter 9.

The purpose of Figure 3.3 is to show the large effect of a ground-coupled thermal mass wall without insulation on the north side of the room that is exposed to the room. This north-side wall was ground filled to its entire height on the outside and not insulated, so that the internal temperature of this wall was nearly a constant 15.5°C (60°F). This north-facing thermal wall had a significant tempering effect on the master bedroom temperatures. For example, as shown in Figure 3.3, with cold outside air far below 10°C (50°F), the interior minimum air temperature of this room rarely dropped below 15.5°C (60°F). This is the result of ground-coupling of this wall. As the outside temperature began to drop in winter starting in October, the master bed room minimum temperature began to drop too; however, it became more steady around 15.5°C (60°F) that was the deep ground temperature. This is quite significant since it requires much less energy to heat the room up from 15.5°C (60°F) to a pleasant room temperature rather than heat it up from the much colder outside temperature.

This ground-coupling effect can be shown even during more short-term periods. Figure 3.4 shows the daily temperatures for the month of January covering the lows, highs, and average. It can be noted that the interior air temperature was nearly a constant 15°C (59°F) over most of the month, when the outside temperature ranged from below freezing point to 7.8°C (46°F) and above. On the coldest day (January 4) the minimum temperature was 1.7°C (29°F) while the inside temperature was 13.3°C (56°F). For this case, the Micropas computer model predicted 15.5°C (60°F). So the ground-coupled thermal mass is a well-understood phenomenon and easily predicted by the computer simulation models.

Finally, it should be pointed out in Figure 3.5 that the coupling of the cold-thermal mass wall could be controlled by insulated sliding doors that cover the wall. Another control method is to have the cold-thermal wall inside a closet that can be closed off from the main room when desired. In the

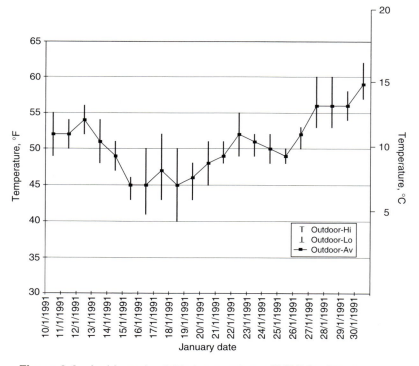

Figure 3.4   Inside and outside temperature of MBR for January.

Berkeley house, the wall ran through a bathroom and several closets and therefore could be closed off while the room was heated during winter. But during summer, this wall kept the room temperature very pleasant through the hottest days without having to resort to any refrigerated air conditioning with high-energy consumption.

3.5   PASSIVE SOLAR HOME – PUTTING TOGETHER THE SOLAR EFFECTS

Figure 3.5 shows how all these solar heating and ground-coupling thermal mass heating/cooling mechanisms discussed above fit together to make the passive solar house work through winter and summer throughout the year.

The thermal mass phenomena works best when coupled carefully with the solar rays passing through a transparent window falling on the thermal mass for heat storage. In summer when the solar heat is not needed and the sun is located higher overhead, a shadow from the roof overhang cast over the window blocks sunlight from getting in onto the floor. This effect of the sun's position and the roof overhang is clearly shown in Figure 3.5. While in winter when the solar heating is

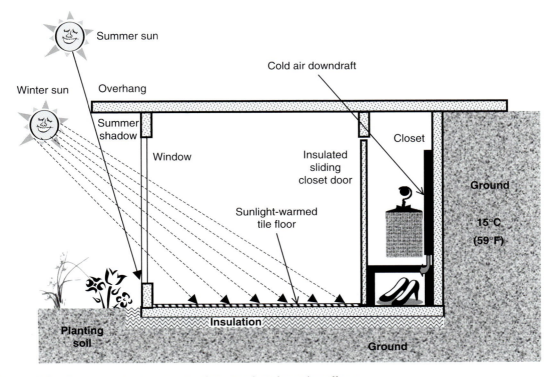

Figure 3.5   Passive solar home – putting together the solar effects.

needed, the tile floor is heated and the heat energy is conducted deep down into the thick concrete slab below. The heat stored in this slab is not conducted away into the cooler ground as there is insulation under this slab and at the edges of the slab exposed to the outside.

The windows on the solar side of the house need to be transparent for the sun's energy to get into the house and also effectively block the infrared re-radiation from inside the house to outside through the windows. These types of solar windows are double or triple paned and have a special layer inside to stop the infrared from leaving. Heat Mirror 77® and 88® are such types available with many window suppliers. These are modeled in the computer codes very well.

In the summer time, when the house does not need heating and the sun rays do not enter the house due to the overhang, additional cooling is also probably needed and the ground-coupled thermal mass serves the purpose very well. Consider the north-side wall of the house as a concrete block or cast concrete that is not insulated from the ground outside with soil backfilling the full height of the wall. A patio or floor up above help keep the moisture from rain. The wall is carefully sealed against the substantial hydrostatic pressure of ground water. The ground soil is very constant at 15°C (59°F). The cold wall creates a cold downdraft on the inside of the house that brings cool air into the room when the insulated sliding doors are opened. A closet can be built next to this wall so that the space can be effectively used and a sliding insulated close door can be used. If this door is mirrored, it helps reflect the winter sunlight scatter light to create a more even illumination.

In the Berkeley house, this ground-coupled north wall configuration was used and it kept the master bedroom pleasantly cool throughout the hottest months of summer. In wintertime, this wall remained at 15°C (59°F) and never dropped to the colder air temperatures outside. No additional insulation was needed against this ground-coupled north wall in winter since the ground temperatures were moderate.

Now that the important mechanisms that are involved in putting these various solar effects and the thermal mass ground-coupling are studied, creative variations are possible to suit one's personal needs.

4

Attached greenhouse passive heating

4.1 SPLIT GREENHOUSE DESIGN

First, we must clarify some terms. A solarium is a sunroom with a large expanse of glass roof and walls that accepts sun and heats the space inside. A solarium can also be a solar greenhouse for plants. So a split greenhouse can have two portions: a solarium and a solar greenhouse. The solarium heats the house and provides a sunny sitting area using the incoming rays from the sun and the solar greenhouse has its interior space heated so that plants can grow well in winter with the extra heating and its hot air can be used to heat the house.

The purpose of the split design is such that the solarium can supply a steady source of heat to the house throughout the year. The energy simulation modeling, discussed earlier, showed a steady heat supply was needed to keep the house at a pleasant living temperature. Various sizes of this fixed section can be examined by the model to find the optimum design.

The solar greenhouse portion is a sealed room that can have its heated air either vented into the house or outside, depending on the house temperature. In addition, this greenhouse can also be used to grow vegetables and start other plants from seed.

Figure 4.1   Split greenhouse design from the inside of the house.

Figure 4.1 shows this split design from the inside of the house and Figure 4.2 shows an aerial view of the house from outside. In Figure 4.1, it can be noted that the windows from the dining room look out through the solar greenhouse to the outside allowing the view of the San Francisco Bay. These windows also allow sunlight to heat the thermal mass of the dining table as discussed earlier.

4.2   FIXED SECTION – THE SOLARIUM

The solarium is a fixed glass section that admits sunlight into the house to heat the tiled floor, air, and provide a pleasant atmosphere for the members living in the house to sit in the sun and read or talk in a very impressive environment.

The window area was determined by the computer energy simulation code to provide the right amount of solar heat to the house throughout the year. In the summer time, when there is too much heat, shades can be automatically drawn to keep unwanted solar heat from entering the house. Section 2.3 provides a discussion of the results of this heating/cooling

Figure 4.2   Aerial view of solar greenhouse from outside.

simulation with shades up and down in the space. The shades can be automated and/or manually controlled when members of the house want to sit under direct sun and when it is not too hot.

The glass type used in this space is Heat Mirror 88® which allows sunlight to pass through efficiently but blocks the re-radiation of the infrared heat energy from escaping to the outside. There is no overhang or designed shading of glass as part of the house outside. It receives the morning sun just after sunrise and continues to receive sunlight all day until sunset. This solarium fixed section is a very significant source of heat for the house.

In order to establish a baseline of performance for the house, the first tests involved the heating and cooling of the house using only the solarium and ventilation, using no active elements through the summer and winter seasons. Figure 4.3 shows a typical day's performance on March 26 when the outside temperature varied from 7.8°C to 11.7°C (46°F to 53°F). The solar flux was measured by Kipp & Zonen pyranometer (Model CM3-L). The effects of the solar heating are

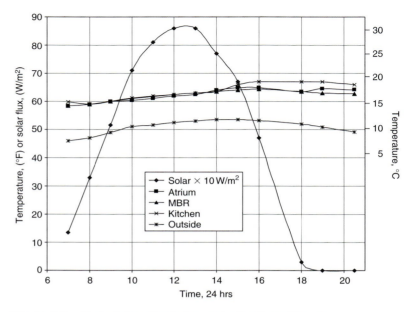

Figure 4.3   Typical day of solarium solar heating of house.

clearly shown in the temperatures of the atrium, master bed-room (MBR), and kitchen starting early in the morning at 14.7°C (58.5°F) and increasingly heating to 17°C (62.5°F) at noon. Then in the afternoon, when the solar heating begins to decline, the rate of temperature increase is not so rapid and begins to steady out to reach a maximum of 17.8°C (64°F) downstairs to 20°C (68°F) in the kitchen upstairs. At night these temperatures decrease only slightly, owing to the substantial temperature storage in the thermal mass throughout the house. This thermal response to solar heating is entirely expected by the transient heating during the solar day. The computer sim-ulation model, MicroPas4, predicted these transients very well.

For the range of cold summer months from January through March, Figure 4.4 shows the average master bedroom tem-perature versus the minimum outdoor temperature. In the upper portion of the plot, the weather type observed for that day is shown.

As discussed earlier in Chapter 03, Figure 3.3 shows data for a whole summer season from June to the end of October where the unshaded solarium provided heating sufficient to maintain the master bedroom average temperature at 24.4°C (76°F). The controls functioning at this point of time were noc-turnal cooling bringing cool air at night. This combination of solarium heating and nocturnal cooling under computer control is the major operational function of this combination. The control aspects are discussed in Chapters 7–9.

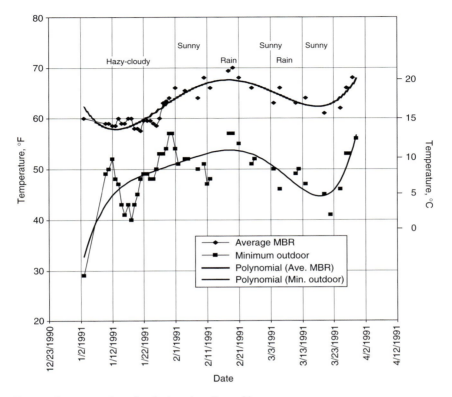

Figure 4.4   Three winter months of solarium heating of house.

Over a whole year, the house without solar shading was found to maintain a consistently pleasant temperature from 16.7°C to 27.8°C (62°F to 82°F), with the peak outdoor temperature records of 38°C (100°F) for several days and 32°C (90°F) for a week-long period.

4.3 CONTROLLED VENT SECTION – THE SOLAR GREENHOUSE

The illustration of the thermal performance of the greenhouse is shown in Figure 4.5 by thermal measurements made in the concrete storage slabs, using a pair of floor thermistor temperature sensors to determine the vertical temperature gradient. One floor sensor was 50 mm (2 inches) below the floor surface and the other 100 mm (4 inches) below. The data shows that the slab picks up heat to reach around 25°C (76°F) at 5 pm by which time the air temperature drops below the concrete temperature. At this point, the heat stored in the slab is released into the greenhouse air space, where this warm air stimulates plant growth and can be used for space heating.

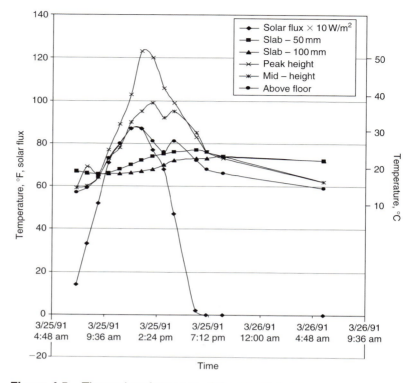

Figure 4.5   Thermal performance of the greenhouse.

By 4:30 am the next day, the outside air temperature had dropped to 10°C (50.1°F), compared to the greenhouse temperature of 15°C (60°F).

Preliminary calculations with these data were performed, which, for brevity will not be detailed, to illustrate the potential value of this kind of instrumentation. The apparent heat transfer coefficient using a surface $\Delta T = 5°C$ or 10°F from air to concrete calculates as 12 W/m²-°C (2 Btu/hr-ft²-°F). It can be noted that this vertical gradient in the concrete reaches a maximum of about 0.05°C/mm or 30°F/ft at a solar flux of 880 W/m², while the vertical thermal stratification in the air is about 0.08°C/mm or 44°F/ft. The thermal conductivity ratio of air to concrete is around 40 – much larger than the temperature gradient ratio. So the heating of the floor appears to be a combination of heat convection and radiation. A slight circulation of the air in the greenhouse would help reduce the thermal stratification with height and would also improve the heat storage down into the slab.

Pairs of temperature sensors spaced just below a thermal storage floor slab are suggested to be used as standard instrumentation in future passive designs to permit comparisons to other buildings on their heat storage ability using this important solar component – the solar greenhouse.

Two other tests were done on the greenhouse on April 9 and 23, 1995 on a clear sunny day with a solar insolation rate of 903 W/m^2 and 934 W/m^2, respectively. With all the circulation to and from the house cut off and the greenhouse vent fan turned off, the temperature reached 49°C (120°F) and 54°C (130°F), respectively for these two days. However, with the external vent fan cooling in the control loop, the temperature was tempered to 35°C (95°F) for an outdoor temperature of 14.4°C (58°F) and 19.4°C (67°F), respectively.

This illustrates that the greenhouse can provide both house heating and plant growing temperatures at the same time. During hot summer days, the temperatures can rise to 60°C (140°F), so the upper vent fan and automatic shades will reduce these high temperatures that are not conducive to ordinary plants in a greenhouse over the summer.

4.4   VEGETABLES

The greenhouse was heated from 27°C to 38°C (80°F to 100°F) from 10 am to 7 pm during the day, regardless of the outside temperature. Since the sloped glass roof and windows had Heat Mirror 88®, the solar efficiency was extremely high and the infrared heat loss was very low as can be seen in Figure 4.5. The greenhouse was designed for providing space heating for the house and no particular design changes were made to accommodate vegetables or other plants.

When the greenhouse was first installed and without an active control system, it remained sealed off from the house for weeks together and temperatures often exceeded 58°C (137°F). As an experiment, some planter boxes were placed in the greenhouse to test the growth of lettuce and tomatoes. The plants did not do well and hence some samples were taken to a local nursery to see if they needed fertilizer or different watering. An experienced horticulturist who had managed commercial greenhouses examined the plants. The following is a conversation with the horticulturist about watering: Okay there was plenty of water. Fertilizer: MiracleGro plant food was excellent. She was very mystified. Then she asked one last critical question: What temperature does the greenhouse reach when the sun is shining on the plants. I answered 58°C (137°F). She looked very disgusted and said: "Shame on you, that is way too high for plants, you should know better than that." Okay, lesson one learned the hard way, by strong embarrassment.

Few months later when the vents were installed and electrical power was turned on, so that the powered vents were functional, more planter boxes were placed in the greenhouse and a variety of vegetables such as lettuce, tomatoes, melons, squash, strawberries, spices, etc. were grown – covering a wide range of varieties to determine which ones were best. The peak temperatures were limited by a ceiling fan control, achieving 27°C to 48°C (80°F to 120°F). But most of these vegetable plants did not do well. The lettuce "bolted" after about a month and tasted bitter. Many of the others just wilted and dried up, despite excess watering.

The following conclusions were drawn after several growing seasons, trying different vegetables, planting month, water cycles, and temperature control:

1. Plant seeds as early as possible in the year, since these handle the heat better than small seedling plants.
2. Adjust the drip water system for 4 am in the morning and 7 pm at night for 10 minutes. Fine spray seemed to prevent the plant from withering under intense sunlight and high temperatures.
3. Chicken manure was the best fertilizer worked into either MiracleGro or EarthGro potting soil for vegetables or flowers.
4. The planter box should be about 500 mm (10″ deep) and elevated to receive light from the front as well as the top. There must be a drain in the box at its lowest point to avoid flooding plant roots. The box can be coated inside with heavy latex paint sealer or roofing tar.
5. The following vegetables did very well in the planter boxes:
   • Swiss chard and regular chard.
   • Carrots – all varieties
   • Kale
   • Potatoes – small size varieties
   • Some hardy varieties of lettuce, like Red sails
6. Cherry tomatoes did very well but down at floor level where peak temperatures were never high and some shade was present for the development of the fruit. Cherry tomatoes could be harvested twice a week for a whole year. The greenhouse can supply several green salads everyday for most of the year, by just snipping, with kitchen scissors, the oldest outer leaves of the lettuce and ripping cherry tomatoes.

Figure 4.6 shows the vegetables harvested to make a huge pot of "Minestrone solar soup" every two weeks. The following ingredients make about 6 liters (1.5 gallons) of soup.

2 cans (220 gms (8 oz)) of Chili concarne without beans
2 cans (1.5 liter (3 pounds)) of chicken stock (fat free or 1% fat)
½ cup (125 cc) converted instant rice
1 cup (250 cc) diced carrots
1 cup (250 cc) diced potato
220 gms (8 oz) packages of frozen vegetables

(continued)

Figure 4.6   Photo of the vegetable harvest.

5 cc garlic salt
Pepper shaken to suit your taste.
Simmer on low heat, covered, for 1 hour with stirring on the bottom every 10 minutes.

Since the chard grew very well all year and was very prolific, we had to develop a recipe of "Cream of chard soup" was made:

Ingredients:
    2 tablespoons (45 mL) butter or margarine or olive oil
    4 cups (1000 mL) chopped chard (leaves and stalks)
    ½ cup (450 mL) chopped green onions
    2 cups (400 gms) diced potatoes or rice
    3 liters (6 pounds) chicken broth
    2 teaspoons (2.5 mL) thyme
    1 teaspoon (2.5 mL) parsley
    ¼ teaspoon (2.5 mL) dill
    ½ cup (125 mL) milk or whipping cream
    ¼ cup (60 mL) chopped chard leaves or green onions to decorate
                                                            (*continued*)

Preparation:
In a large pot, melt butter over low heat or use olive oil
Mix in chopped chard stalks (not leaves) and green onions
Sauté while stirring over low heat until diced stalks and onions are tender
Add potatoes or rice, chicken broth, and stir
Bring to a boil, then reduce heat and simmer for 30 minutes
Add diced chard leaves, thyme, parsley, and dill
Cook for additional 10 minutes
Remove from heat and let cool slightly
Add milk or cream and stir
Puree in a blender or food processor (or immerse Braun turbo blender) and reheat
Garnish with parsley and/or diced green onions and serve hot.

This Cream of chard soup is particularly good when extra rich whipped cream is used with rice or without rice. However, it is very easy when the Braun turbo-blender is used right in the pot. The latter eliminates the risk of handling batches of hot soup in a separate blender or food processor. Except for the small amount of cream and the chicken broth, all the ingredients can be grown in the solar greenhouse.

Figure 4.7 shows the greenhouse with the elevated planter box 0.6 m wide $\times$ (5 m long (24" wide $\times$ 16' long) and some smaller drip system pots for lettuce varieties. The planter box was sloped to the drain and had a single drain that was plumbed into the sewer line through a J-trap.

Experience with this greenhouse for growing vegetables has been extremely successful with a drip water system. However, further improvement can be recommended to install a storm drain so that the floor can be washed down by hose for removal of dirt and mud.

4.5   STARTING EARLY SEED PLANTS

The solar greenhouse was found to be ideal for starting early plants from seeds. A large improvement in plant growth and productivity can be observed when grown from seed. It was found that when nursery plants were brought into the solar greenhouse and planted, they were significantly harmed by the stress of high heat levels inside the greenhouse when it was also used for solar heating of the home.

When plants were grown from seed, they seemed to be much better acclimatized to the hot environment of the greenhouse. While the nursery plants wilted in high heat, the plants grown from seed never wilted.

Figure 4.7   Photo of the greenhouse with the elevated planter box.

The elevated planter box described above was placed under the overhang from the dining room windows just above the planter box. Recessed in this overhang are a series of Grow Lamps, with special fluorescent tubes that better simulated sunshine spectral distribution. These lights were placed on timers so that the day was artificially lengthened to spring time days even though it was late winter with little sun. The added light and warmth from the sun, very quickly stimulated the seeds to germinate and start small seedling plants. Typically two weeks were sufficient for a plant to start. Each plant variety started over a different time period.

Planting the seeds was very easy. A long batten board 5 mm thick × 45 mm high × 2.5 m long (¼" thick × 2" high × 8' long) was simply pushed down into the fresh soil to make a small, long dent in the soil about 7 mm (⅜") deep. Into this dent, seeds were carefully sprinkled out of their paper envelopes. It was important to sprinkle them slowly with a little vibration on the envelope so that the seeds were properly spaced out per instructions on the envelope. Great care and dexterity were needed to perform this sprinkling well and not have clumps of seeds overlapping. After the seeds were distributed along this dent, a light brushing with the hand over the dent covered the seeds by about 5 mm (¼") of fine soil.

A fine mist spray was sufficient to keep the soil wet without heavy water flows to dislodge the seeds. The mist watering was done twice a day for 10 minutes at about 4 am and again at about 7 pm, when it was cooler in the greenhouse. For extreme summer heat the water times could be increased to 20 minutes.

The spacing of the rows with different varieties of plants was also important. For example, in the back row the taller plants, like chard, worked well with the smaller plants like carrots in front where their foliage could hang over the front of the planter box for sunlight, without shading the plants behind. Lettuce did best in the pole pots, but could also be placed along the front row, as long as it was not over-crowded by carrots.

Productivity in the solar greenhouse was very impressive. Two rows of carrots from four packages of seeds, was sufficient for nearly a whole year with soup everyday for a family of three. Chard and Kale stalks could be snipped with kitchen scissors to produce a big handful in less than a minute.

The pole pots also worked well for a variety of herbs, since the pot elevation was an important variable that provided the variation in temperature and shading that some needed. Also these pots could be removed from the pole and repositioned to different heights or moved to another pole. These pole pots can be seen in Figure 4.7.

Of course, all during the growing and harvesting of vegetables and herbs the solar greenhouse provides space heating for the house. Screens are used to prevent any insects living in the vegetables getting into the house. The added humidity from the greenhouse can be an advantage since it helps the heat in the house feel more livable. The air also has a slight earthy smell of green plants, which is also a positive aspect. Thus, the solar home dweller feels closer to nature and is being kind to the environment as well. One has to experience the enjoyment of a solar greenhouse, for the satisfaction of "solar living."

Domestic hot water

5.1   HOUSE DHW USAGE PATTERNS

The term DHW is used all over the world to mean "domestic hot water" and does not include hot water for space heating. In addition, DHW historically has been the first large scale application of solar energy since 1940s in Florida. Simple thermal collectors for DHW were developed and sold 50 years earlier than PV collectors.

The normally accepted US consumption of energy to provide DHW is 15.9 GJ/year (Duffie and Beckman, 1991) and does not change significantly month-to-month. In the Berkeley house, the solar energy used to heat the DHW was 3.4 GJ/year. Figure 5.1 shows the photo of the hot water heater in this house. About 38% of this energy was a heat loss from the hot water tank; thus about 2.08 GJ/year was actually used in DHW.

The solar-provided DHW system is rather unique and produces 99% of the domestic needs for hot water. It uses the same solar thermal collectors as for swimming pool heating and for space heating.

For the 1% of the year that the DHW requires auxiliary heating, a 5.8 kW electrical heater is used. It would also be possible to supply this 1% from the topping heat exchanger of the heat pump.

This 99% DHW system storage capacity is comparable to the hot water tanks (200–300 L) used extensively in Northern

Figure 5.1   Photo of hot water heater in Berkeley solar house.

Europe which achieve only 90% of the solar house's domestic hot water needs.

5.2   DHW TANK STORAGE CAPACITY

The stainless steel, 545 L (120 gallon) solar water heater tank with integral heat exchanger was built by TAM Tanks of Canada. Stainless steel was selected so that it need not be replaced because of its unique design in both large size and the heat exchanger coils that heat this tank with solar-heated glycol.

Hot water from this tank would be used down to 46°C (115°F). This temperature was selected because the shower hot water mixing valve in the shower would be at the fully hot position with the water temperature pleasantly hot for showering. After 30 minutes of total showering, no noticeable drop in hot water temperature could be detected since the measured temperature drop in tank water temperature was only 1.6°C (3°F).

A typical cycle to recharge and boost the hot water tank back to 63°C (145°F) takes about 3.5 hours in sunny weather in the wintertime. This short thermal recharge cycle allows the hot solar collectors to dump their excess heat into the pool and continue to heat the pool normally. Pool heating will be covered in Chapter 7.

The selection of this higher temperature of 63°C (145°F) was found to be a very important parameter. There is a tradeoff between frequent recharge periods but shorter recharge times, against longer recharge times which can exceed one winter solar heating day. Not being able to recharge the hot water tank within one solar day was found to be very wasteful. For instance, on the first day the hot water would be close to its final temperature, but when the sun angle became low the solar thermal collectors did not operate efficiently at their highest temperatures. The recharge operation at near peak temperatures at the end of a solar day required a long time. Then at the end of the solar day, not having completed the hot water recharge, the solar collectors at their peak temperatures were then shut down, wasting the substantial amount of collected solar heat. It was noted that since more heat loss from the tank occurred during cool nights and the fact that there is no sun, concludes that the recharge cycle mostly started in the morning when the sun was up and strong.

Also the intermittent nature of cloudy weather is another important factor. It was found that during rainstorms, there are short periods during storms when there is sunlight for 4 hours or so. Recharge cycle during this short period of sun during storms is sufficient to completely recharge the hot water. In this way, about 99% hot water supply heated by solar heat was possible, which was accomplished even without the extremely large hot water storage tanks normally used in solar systems.

It was found to be most efficient when the recharge cycle started in the morning and completed the cycle about 1 hour after the solar noon, when the solar collectors normally reached their maximum temperature, which meant a recharge cycle of about 4–5 hours. So this fixes the optimum upper temperature, which was found to be 63°C (145°F). The details of the automatic control to accomplish these solar DHW tank recharge cycles are covered in Section 5.6.

In scaling up this solar hot water system in size, it is recommended to maintain the 4–5 hours of recharge cycle. So to meet the larger hot water use, scaling up the solar thermal collectors and the hot water storage tanks in proportion is necessary.

Another advantage of the short recharge cycle is that the sensitive heat stored in the thermal collectors, the high glycol heat and the hot copper piping will be dumped into the swimming pool at the end of the recharge cycle. In this way, the system efficiency for the combined DHW and the swimming pool is particularly high. This synergy is discussed in more detail in Chapter 7.

The hot water tank contains tap water that is replenished by cold tap water at the lowest level, and the heated DHW leaves from the top of the tank where it is the hottest. There is substantial thermal stratification of the heated water in this tank and temperature sensors located from the bottom, middle, and top show at least 10°C (18°F) temperature differences. This stratification was found to be an advantage, actually, since when the tank is only partially heated, the hottest water is delivered to the house for use. So that the very last volume of hot water can be used while the tank is being recharged. Therefore, mixing the tanks is not recommended.

For applications that do not have a swimming pool and any other place to dump the excess heat, special high-pressure considerations must be fixed, to prevent the build up of steam, by means of a pressure diaphragm expansion tanks to handle the expansion of the glycol with temperature. This is called solar thermal collector "stagnation." An emergency pressure relief valve at the highest point on the top collector is required to avoid pressure extremes beyond the rating of the thermal collectors.

Lastly, a comparison should be made with the *f*-chart analysis method (Duffie and Beckmann, 1991). Following this method, "Y" is calculated as the ratio of the absorbed solar energy from the thermal collectors to the DHW load. Next "X" is calculated as the ratio of reference collector loss to the DHW load. From these two parameters, a prediction is made of the percentage of solar energy utilization in heating DHW. The results for the large hot water tank and the 8 Heliodyne (Gobi model) solar thermal collectors totaling $23.8\,m^2$ ($256\,ft^2$) produce a solar utilization factor, *f* that is well over 90% and close to 99%, with Y ranging from 4.9 for a bad weather solar year to 7.0 for an average year and X about 5. The results of the *f*-chart method for liquid systems are shown in Figure 20.3.1 of Duffie and Beckmann (1991). Of course, this surprising result stems from the fact that the area of the solar thermal collectors is tremendously larger than normally designed for

DHW alone. They were designed to provide swimming pool heating but can also be used for DHW with only a change in valve position whenever needed. The combination of these two solar loads is very advantageous and discussed in Chapter 7.

5.3 PLUMBING CONFIGURATION

The piping arrangement has been shown schematically in Figure 5.2. On the upper left is an array of glazed, black copper Heliodyne (Gobi model) solar thermal collectors being illuminated by the sun. They are pitched at a 45° angle with an azimuth about 6° west of south to capture a little more of the warmer afternoon sun. Glycol–water mixture of about 20% glycol is used to prevent freezing in the wintertime. The system is always filled and does not have a drain down feature. The automatic controls are discussed in more detail in Section 5.6.

Referring to the lower left of Figure 5.2, the magnetic-drive, sealed pump circulates the glycol up into the solar collectors on the roof. The circulation rate for a series system of 8 Heliodyne collectors, 1 m × 2.43 m (3 ft × 8 ft) each is about

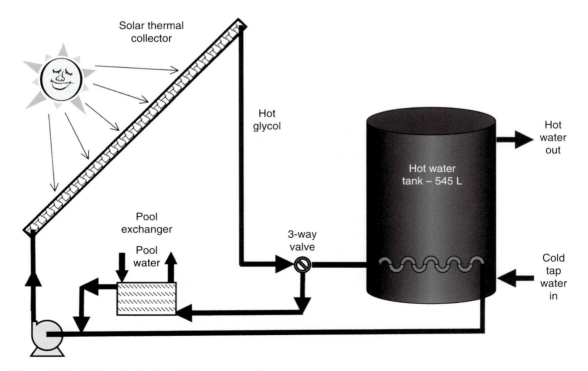

Figure 5.2 Hot water heater piping schematic.

36 L/minutes (8 gpm). The solar-heated hot glycol at temperatures up to 110°C (230°F) exits the collectors and travels down through well-insulated 50-mm (2-inch) copper pipes to a 3-way automatic valve 7 m (22 ft) below in the hot water heater room at the ground floor. The position of this 3-way valve is controlled by the temperature of the water in the hot water tank. If its temperature is below 46°C (115°F), then the hot glycol is circulated through the stainless steel (double wall) heat exchanger in the hot water tank. The hot glycol continues to heat the hot water tank until its temperature reaches 63°C (145°F), at which point the 3-way valve diverts the hot glycol through the swimming pool heat exchanger located in the garage machine room. This heat exchanger must be a proper alloy to handle hot chlorine-containing pool water. Cupro-Nickel used for marine applications is required. It might be possible to use some of the stainless steels high in nickel content, like 316-L, but caution is well warranted. Earlier conventional plate heat exchanger which corroded to destruction in 9 years was used. However, now shell-in-tube phosphor bronze Heliodyne unit was installed. The latter is fitted with a sacrificial anode to protect against galvanic-induced corrosion.

It was found that a large hot water tank with many large diameter pipe penetrations of thermally conductive copper to and from the tank were a cause of significant heat loss. To estimate the magnitude of this effect, we used the experimentally measured heat loss data (see Section 5.4) to calculate the heat transfer coefficient of 1.13 W/m²-°C. This is significantly higher than for conventional solar hot water tanks that have about 0.62 W/m²-°C. Comparison of copper piping with a thermal conductivity of 386 W/m-°C against a thermal conductivity of 16 W/m-°C for 316-L stainless steel illustrates the large advantage of using short length of stainless steel piping for these penetrations.

The hot water tank has five pipe penetrations: two for the internal heat exchanger, two for DHW in and out, and one for pressure relief. The pipes are 25 mm diameter with 1 mm wall, so that the cross-sectional area of copper is 79 mm² and an average length of 150 mm (6") from the hot water to the outside air heat sink. For this case, the heat conduction loss totals 33 W or 1.1 GJ/year. The DHW use averages from 3 to 10 GJ/year for the Berkeley house and the US average house draws about 15 GJ/year. So the fraction of DHW energy that is wasted in piping conduction heat loss varies from 30% in the DHW conserving case down to 7% in the typical US house.

The thermal conductivity of hot water is 0.66 W/m-°C; therefore, by dropping the piping conductivity below water gains very little, since the pipes are normally filled with water in use. The conductive heat loss from the water inside the pipes is only 1% of the heat conduction loss from copper piping.

Therefore, using short lengths of stainless steel piping could drop these metal conduction losses down to 0.04 GJ/year and from water in the pipe to 0.09 GJ/year. So now the percentage loss is dropped from 5% to 1%, respectively.

If there were heavy gauge plastic piping that would handle the high temperatures, they typically have a thermal conductivity as low as 0.2 W/m-°C. However, for this situation, the water conduction would clearly dominate the heat loss and going to a plastic section would not be justified.

5.4   INSULATION

Effective insulation around a tank is very important. This large tank has four standard hot water heat blankets installed on top of each other to achieve 100 mm (4") of fiberglass insulation. The tank is set on 50 mm (2") fiberboard insulation to eliminate conduction through the bottom of the tank. The additional insulation is applied to the outside of the tank, which already has about the same amount of insulation inside the sheet metal enclosure. This added thick insulation is shown in Figure 5.1.

With the extra amount of insulation, the heat loss data and hot water draw down during different DHW use have been gathered as shown in Figure 5.3. It should be noted that under the recharge cycle selected, there is a 2-day capacity of hot water with both heat loss and DHW usage patterns. A typical hot water usage rate of a given day depletes the stored temperature by about 1.6°C (3°F). This depletion pattern can be seen in the data looking at daily patterns over a full week of use. The difference between the two series of data, LCD and LCD-V shows this depletion. During periods of extra heavy hot water use, there are several incidences showing data points below the lowest series at about double the temperature depletion of 3.3°C (6°F).

During the initial period of heat loss of 0.4 days, just after the fully recharged heating up to 63°C (147°F), the heat loss is about half the rate of that after 0.6 days. This lower heat loss regime during the initial period is believed to arise from the fact that the heat exchanger metals, piping, structure etc. were all at a higher temperature than the water in order to transfer heat into the water. Upon completion of the recharge cycle, the metals are no longer hotter than the water since its heat has been transferred to the water and the heat transfer is now out of the heater into the surrounding air.

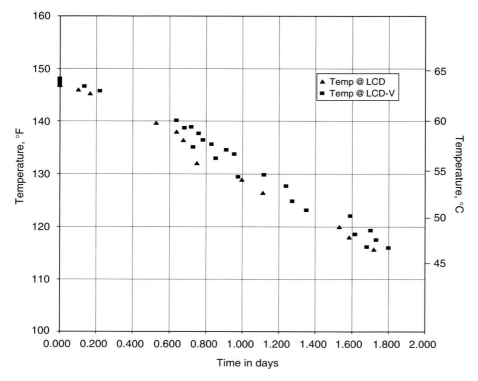

Figure 5.3   Heat loss from hot water heater.

After this initial heat loss period, the heat loss decay rate is very linear, noted by the near linear decay curves from 0.6 days down to 1.8 days. It is believed that this heat loss is now controlled by the temperature driving force, as the temperature difference between the hot water inside the tank and that of the air outside the tank and the tank-enclosed room. For example, at the 0.6-day point the driving force for heat loss would be about 42°C (75°F), while that at the end of the heat loss would be about 28°C (50°F). This slight change is a little hard to see in the data.

If one were to select a much higher hot water temperature for recharge, say 75°C (167°F), then the DHW use period would be expected to be lengthened from 2 days to about 3.2 days. In fact, during the initial set up and checking period for the DHW operation, the higher recharge temperature was used. Under this higher temperature scenario, the recharge cycle generally could not be completed in one day except during the extended solar days of summer. Therefore, the longer recharge cycle was less efficient and did not take advantage of brief period of cloud clearing during and between rainstorms or typical foggy summer conditions. Of course, different solar homeowners may want to experiment with different recharge scenarios to find the optimum for their own location's weather type.

5.5   TEMPERATURE MONITORING LOCATIONS

The locations of the temperature sensors on the hot water tank are very important. There is substantial thermal stratification of the heated water in this tank and temperature sensors located from the bottom, middle, and top show at least 10°C (18°F) temperature differences and sometimes more.

This stratification results from the colder, denser water remaining at the bottom and the warmer water on the top. When the tank is only partially heated, the hottest water is delivered to the house for use. So that the last volumes of hot water can be used while the tank is being recharged. The dynamics of this thermal stratification are not simple, as seen from experience with the tank.

Installing thermistors at different locations on the tank wall is very easy, since they can be simply glued on by epoxy placing the thermistor carefully and then completely covering with insulation. Locating the thermal sensors on the outer surface of this stainless tank wall does not contribute a significant error, especially when they are insulated very well. Thermistors are available in various types, they come as buttons, short cylinders, and cylinders with a flat tab. Its metal casing is copper so that the heat is rapidly conducted to the sensitive resistor inside. The technology is very mature and cost less. Goldline is one of the distributors of these sensors. The types used for Berkeley house were all of the $10\,k\Omega$ variety. The conversion of their resistance with temperature change is accomplished by the controller so that a temperature output digital result is displayed.

The thermistors were found to be very precise. A number of different constant temperature baths had been prepared into which they could be submersed to check the precision of many thermistors to insure they worked correctly. With careful wiring connections to insure good solid contacts, the temperatures could be reliably read out with ±0.01°C (±0.02°F) display resolution. The extra decimal digits are displayed as they are very important in observing small changes in temperature to note whether a particular location is experiencing heating or cooling. This extra capability is extremely helpful in solar systems and does not cost more.

By examining the transition between the hot upper layer and the cold lower layer, one can get an idea of how much hot water is in the tank that could be drawn off. More thermal sensors would help the resolution of the location of this thermocline and is recommended for those homeowners interested in this important solar technology.

5.6   CONTROLS

The hot water is initially stored at 63°C (145°F) as a result of being heated by 105°C (221°F) hot glycol generated in the solar collectors. As the hot water is consumed and the temperature decreases to 46°C (115°F), the swimming pool pump is switched off and no longer circulates cool pool water through the pool heat exchanger. The solar collector quickly increases in temperature so that it can now produce the domestic hot water. A typical cycle to recharge and boost the hot water tank back to 63°C (145°F) takes only 3.5 hours in sunny weather, after which the hot solar collectors dump their excess heat into the pool and continue to heat the pool normally.

Figure 5.4 shows a control wiring schematic for hot water heater. There are three temperature-indicating controllers (TIC) although they could be combined into a more complex controller. These controllers are supplied by Goldline[1] with their model numbers depicted in the figure.

At the lower left of Figure 5.4 the controller, CM-30, is a comparative controller and examines the difference in

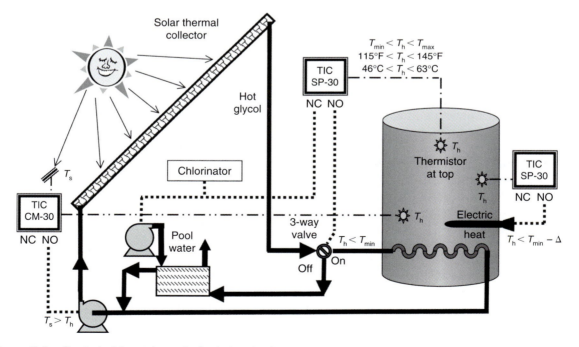

Figure 5.4   Control wiring schematic for hot water heater.

temperature between the solar sensor, T_s, and the hot water temperature, T_h, measured at the lower location where the water is the coldest. The solar sensor – commercially available from suppliers like Heliodyne and others – consists of a copper thermal mass circular plate on which is attached a temperature-measuring thermistor. This plate is under a glass cover and well insulated at the sides and back. It responds to sunlight by heating the plate slowly. In this manner it does not respond to small clouds passing over and has a thermal lag of the order of 10 minutes.

When the temperature of this solar sensor, T_s, is higher than the lower hot water temperature, T_h, the controller starts the solar thermal collector circulation pump. For the system of 8 Gobi collectors, the pump circulates at 45 L/minutes (12 gpm). There is also a rotometer flowmeter indicating this flowrate. This is important in insuring that there are no flow restrictions, the pump is operating correctly, and the valves are operating.

In the upper center of Figure 5.4, there is a second controller SP-30 which is a single point controller. It examines the temperature, T_h, at the top of the hot water tank. When the tank is colder then it has a minimum set-point, T_{min}, and the controller positions the 3-way value so that the hot glycol from the solar thermal collectors passes through the hot water tank coils at the bottom. When the tank is heated to its maximum set-point, T_{max}, then the 3-way valve is repositioned to send the hot glycol to the swimming pool heat exchanger. The temperature, T_h, is displayed on the wall-mounted color touch screen showing all house systems, which will be discussed in later chapters. In addition to this controller sending the hot glycol to the swimming pool heat exchanger, it also runs the large swimming pool circulation pump as well as the electrochemical chlorinator, which will be discussed in later chapters.

For the 1% of the year that the DHW requires auxiliary heating, an electrical heater is used. This heater is turned on by a separate thermostat, SP-30 at the right side of Figure 5.4 set at about 42°C (110°F) to insure no overlap. It would also be possible to supply this 1% from the topping heat exchanger of the heat pump.

There are many choices made by taking advantage of the recharge cycle while using hot water in a house. For example, by scheduling a large wash during a recharge cycle, allows this hot water to be available when the heating can be the most efficient. When these large hot water demands are made during a recharge cycle, when one is done, the DHW tank is left in the fully charged, hottest condition and not partially depleted.

One improvement in automatic control would be recommended. When the hot water tank is at an intermediate temperature somewhat lower than the maximum 63°C (145°F) but above the minimum 46°C (115°F), then it would be helpful to manually trigger a recharge cycle. The reason for this manual intervention over the automatic controls is the anticipation of a heavy 3-day foggy, cloudy or rainy condition that was expected soon. Supposing that the DHW temperature in the tank is 50°C (124°F) and would probably fall below the minimum acceptable hot water temperature when bad weather arrives and the sun is lost, then triggering an early recharge, the few hours of sun (approximately 2 hours) that is available before bad weather, can be used to fully recharge the hot water. In this way, the solar house hot water tank will be fully charged to 63°C (145°F) even in bad weather.

Automating the above bad weather anticipatory actions are presently attempted using a standard weather monitor (such as those supplied by Davis Instruments). This early DHW recharge can simply be triggered by switching in series with the thermistor a 2500-ohm resistor that makes the temperature look like 20°C (35°F) cooler than it is. This starts the recharge cycle early. It can be switched back once the recharge is underway and the controller system will continue to function as before. The weather monitors, such as Davis Instrument, Model Vantage PRO®, will soon provide a relay closure upon the amount of barometric pressure fall, which anticipates an incoming storm at least 3 hours ahead and perhaps more. One can select up to four alarm conditions for triggering and select alarms from two different weather parameters. An ideal combination would be to look for a falling barometer only after the barometer gets below a certain low reading or combined with outside high humidity or wind speed. The idea is to try tuning this added logic in the weather monitor to anticipate an incoming storm or clouds in the most accurate manner.

ENDNOTE

1. They are normally distributed by HVAC supply houses and are around US $100 each. They are very small and compact and wall surface mounted. Also, simple to install and use, and they come with excellent documentation. They have never failed in the Berkeley house and are very robust.

6

Combined DHW and swimming pool heating

6.1 SYNERGISTIC RELATIONSHIP

There are many synergies gained by combining the heating of DHW with the larger number of solar thermal collectors, needed for swimming pool heating. First, there is the elimination of added solar thermal collectors and all the plumbing dedicated for DHW. Second, the DHW is produced very quickly. There are a number of advantages of a short DHW recharge cycle such as, dumping excess heat into the swimming pool from hot glycol and sensible heat stored in the thermal collectors, and all the hot copper piping at the end of the recharge cycle. In this way, the system efficiency for the combined DHW and the swimming pool is particularly high.

This combination utilizes the advantage of the intermittent nature of cloudy weather. It was found that during rainstorms, there are short periods during storms when there is sunlight for about 4 hours when the DHW can be recharged. This short period of sunlight during storms is sufficient to completely recharge the hot water. In this way, about 99% hot water supply heated by solar heat was possible, which was accomplished even without the extremely large hot water storage tanks normally used in solar systems.

The most efficient cycle was to start the recharge cycle in the morning and complete the cycle about 1 hour after solar noon, when the solar collectors normally reach their maximum temperature. This means a recharge cycle of about 4–5 hours which fixes the optimum upper temperature, which was found to be 63.9°C (147°F). The details of the automatic control to accomplish these solar DHW tank recharge cycles were already covered in Section 5.6.

In scaling up this solar hot water system in size, it is recommended to maintain the 4–5 hours of short recharge cycle. So it is necessary to scale up the solar thermal collectors and the hot water storage tanks in proportion, to meet the large demand for hot water.

6.2   COLLECTOR CAPACITY

The combined heating of DHW and a swimming pool at the Berkeley solar house dictated that the solar thermal collectors be sized for heating the swimming pool. The upper limit of the number of collectors was determined by the available roof area. The amount of heat they produce, or capacity, is just their efficiency times the solar insolation.

The type of collector also determines its capacity. For example, if only the swimming pool is heated, then a simple black plastic solar collector will serve, since it does not have to reach high temperatures and need not have a glass-covered surface (i.e. glazed) for high efficiency. On the other hand, if higher temperatures are needed for heating domestic water or providing space heating, then a high temperature solar thermal collector is needed with a glass cover to maintain the higher heat. A comparison of the performance between these two types of collectors is shown in Figure 6.1.

In the figure the upper curve is the measured efficiency of the Heliodyne Gobi Model (Heliodyne, 2003), a double-glazed, selective black surface solar thermal collector, as a function of the temperature difference between the glycol coming into the collector, T_{in}, minus the temperature of the ambient air, T_{air}, divided by the solar insolation, I, in W/m^2. Even though the site was extremely windy most of the time, these measurements did not significantly depend on wind velocity.

The lower curve is that of the FAFCO, a black polypropylene plastic, round dimpled tube collector designed for swimming pool heating (FAFCO, 2003). The dimples are placed on the tubes at an angle and depth such that they create a spiral flow of the fluid producing a higher, turbulent heat transfer coefficient that improves their efficiency. Since it was unglazed, the measurements were strongly dependent on the wind velocity. The data shown are for the most quiescent day. Higher

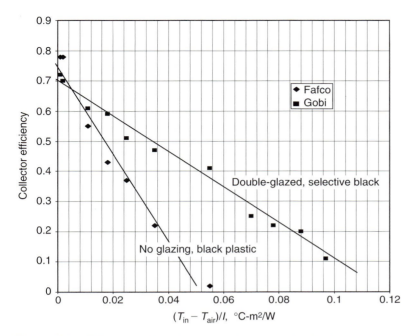

Figure 6.1   Efficiency of two types of solar thermal collector.

wind velocity worsened the heat loss and lowered the efficiency significantly.

From this comparison of solar thermal collectors, one can contrast the efficiencies of the design operating conditions for the swimming pool and DHW. Considering the swimming pool at 25.6°C (78°F) and the ambient temperature at 18°C (64°F) with a solar insolation of 800 W/m², the abscissa group, $(T_{in} - T_{air})/I$, would be 0.013, with efficiencies of about 0.67 for both collectors. However, for DHW in the storage tank at the end of a recharge at 63.9°C (147°F), at the same ambient temperature and insolation, the abscissa group is 0.057 and the efficiencies are 0.38 for the Gobi glazed collector and about zero for the black plastic FAFCO collector. So clearly, heating DHW will require a double-glazed, selective black surface collector, like Heliodyne's Gobi.

It is possible to have both the black plastic collector for the swimming pool and the Gobi for DHW, but the roof area is just not sufficient for all these collectors and also doubles all the piping. It would be cheaper to add an additional Gobi collector and use these collectors for both DHW and swimming pool heating, exactly the decision made for the Berkeley house.

The swimming pool is 4.8 m × 11 m (15 ft × 35 ft) in a kidney-bean shape with a volume of 76,000 liters (20,000 gallons) and covered by a standard blue bubble blanket. The first pool-heating test started with a uniform pool temperature of

13.9°C (57°F). The pool water was heat-exchanged with the solar panel glycol-water mixture in the original compact multi-plate exchanger $0.5\,m^2$ ($5\,ft^2$). On a typical winter day with an outside air temperature of 8.3°C (47°F) and a peak solar inso-lation rate of $400\,W/m^2$, the water temperature was raised by 0.83°C (1.5°F) throughout the day. On a typical spring day with the outside temperature around 21°C (70°F) and a peak solar insolation rate of $700\,W/m^2$, the water temperature was raised by 2.2°C (4°F). These results correlate well with the expected efficiencies of the Heliodyne Gobi solar collectors as given by the manufacturer's efficiency relation:

$$E = 0.7255 - 0.5633 \times \Delta T/I - 0.0022 \times \Delta T^2/I$$

This equation will be very important in the modeling of these Gobi collectors in performance over a wide range of temperature.

When planning a solar house, plans about including a swimming pool or not should be carefully considered or whether it would be added in the future. If collectors are sized only for DHW, it is likely there will not be enough collector area to provide swimming pool heating over a sufficiently long swimming season or enough for space heating (discussed in Chapter 7).

Some discussions about operational warnings are in order. First, there is the safety condition of "stagnation" where the pumps, piping, and/or controls have failed, and there is no flow through the collectors on a hot solar day. This stagnation condition causes the solar collector to reach unacceptably high temperatures. For this condition, there is a pressure relief valve placed at the highest point in the plumbing where the hottest glycol leaves the collectors. The relief pressure set-ting is selected where water boils off at the highest tempera-ture and pressure rating for the collectors. A typical pressure rating for collectors is 6.8 atm. (100 psi) at which pressure water boils at 164°C (327°F). Normally high temperature oper-ating conditions needed to complete the DHW heating recharge at 63.9°C (147°F), on a hottest solar day experienced at the Berkeley house, raises the highest temperature Gobi collector to 131°C (267°F). This condition is shown with the last data point at the lower right in Figure 6.1 with an efficiency of 0.11.

Stagnation conditions should be avoided, since extensive periods of boiling water off a glycol mixture and venting steam concentrates the glycol locally and can cause decom-position deposits that will cause long-term damage to the collector flow passages. Some glycols will decompose more easily than others, and the maximum temperature should be carefully considered when purchasing replacement glycol.

6.3   SWIMMING SEASON AND POOL TEMPERATURE

Even though all the 8 Heliodyne Gobi solar thermal collectors were used to provide 99% of the DHW needs and some weeks of radiant floor heating, there was still plenty of solar heating capacity to provide swimming pool temperatures within an acceptable range from 25°C (77°F) to 34.5°C (92°F) from early April to the end of October – a 7-month swimming season! One more month can be added if the pool is purposely over-heated to extend swimming by two weeks in November and two weeks in March. Of course, such an 8-month swimming pool operation is only possible for climates comparable or warmer than in California, which includes half of the world.

Another strategy can be followed to extend the swimming season. When the swimming pool is overheated reaching 35–40°C (95–104°F) during the hottest weeks of summer, the swimming pool insulating bubble blanket is pulled back to allow some heat loss and cooling during the nights. Instead, the homeowner can trigger an early DHW recharge rather than wasting this valuable solar heat or can allow this higher temperature of the pool water to carry additional heat past the end of summer.

The swimming pool uses a unique electrochemical unit made by Clearwater, an Australian firm, which converts the low level salt content of the water into oxy-chlorine disinfectant. Figure 6.2 shows this electrochemical chlorination cell.

Figure 6.2   Photo of Clearwater solar powered pool chlorinator.

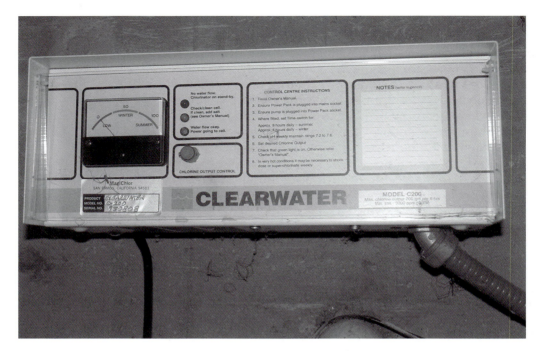

Figure 6.3   Photo of Clearwater chlorinator power supply and control.

Figure 6.3 shows its power supply and controller. In fact, all the chlorination is provided by the PV collectors-supplied electrical power when the sun is shining and the chlorine disinfectant is needed. It works incessantly and flawlessly since it was installed about 7 years ago. The only chemical required to maintain pool water chemistry is the addition of Muriatic acid for pH control. This has been automated with an oxidation reduction potential (ORP) control for chlorine and a pH controller to bleed in small amounts of acid.

6.4   SMART CONTROLS

In Section 5.6 the possible automatic control strategy with bad weather approaching using a standard weather monitor (supplied by Davis Instruments (Davis, 2003)) was discussed. The early DHW recharge was simply triggered by the weather monitor. The weather monitors, such as Davis Instruments, Model Vantage PRO®, provides a trigger upon the amount of barometric pressure fall, which will anticipate an incoming storm at least 3 hours ahead and perhaps more.

In other locations and other countries, there are radio alerts issued for storm warning and the tone can be used to trigger a relay closure that will start the early DHW recharge or other control functions desired.

Another technique using "smart" controls during "peak load" periods of noon to 6 pm is to switch off the swimming pools' large pump used to filter the water. This 1.5 hp pump (0.8 hp at low speed) is the largest electrical load for the house. During hot solar days, of course, the swimming pool is heated by using a portion of the power generated by the solar PV, so some power is still being fed back to the grid for credit. So what can be done for load shifting so that more solar PV can offset electric load during this "on-peak" period and gain a larger credit? One strategy is to make DHW by triggering an early recharge which uses the solar thermal collectors, but switches off the pool pumps. The hardware controls needed to do this are already in place and will be discussed in the space heating/cooling in Chapters 7 and 8, but some creative software programming is needed to trigger DHW recharge starting at noon on weekdays. The simple software calendar capability that is part of the Tridium software can do this. The hardware and software controls are provided by Invensys (2003) and distributed by Siebe Controls (2003) and installed by Yamas Controls (Yamas, 2003).

This load shifting strategy will only work for a few days, and once the DHW is fully charged, it cannot be used. The DHW can be over-heated slightly to increase the temperature above the normal high temperature control set-point (presently, 63.9°C, (147°F)). In the Berkeley house, this concept was tested up to temperatures of 82°C (180°F). So with some creativity and some smart control capability, there are a large number of possible strategies that can be used to save energy, reduce operating costs, and take advantage of load shifting.

6.5 SOLAR PVs TO SUPPLY POWER TO SWIMMING POOL PUMP AND CHLORINATOR

As stated above, the swimming pool uses a unique electrochemical unit made by Clearwater, an Australian firm (Clearwater, 2003), which converts the low level salt content of the water into oxy-chlorine disinfectant. So the disinfectant is provided by solar PV-supplied electrical power when the sun is shining and the oxy-chlorine disinfectant is needed. It works incessantly and flawlessly since it was installed about 7 years ago. The only chemical required to maintain pool water chemistry is the addition of Muriatic acid for pH control. This has been automated with an ORP control for chlorine and a pH controller to bleed in small amounts of acid.

The combined electrical load for the swimming pool pump operating at low speed and the chlorinator, together with the small glycol-circulating pump totals 972 W. This is about half of the solar PV-electrical power provided.

A load/solar PV comparison for December when the received solar energy was the least was made. It should be noted that in the wintertime there is still enough solar PV power to operate the swimming pool filtering and chlorination. This saves the cost of draining the pool, cleaning the pool, refilling it with expensive tap water, adding more chemicals and salt. Also, an empty pool is a danger for little children and animals falling into the ditch. Hence, this strategy for cost saving is well recommended, even though conventional experience would be to drain a swimming pool during winter. This approach of maintaining swimming pool water chemistry throughout the year is highly recommended.

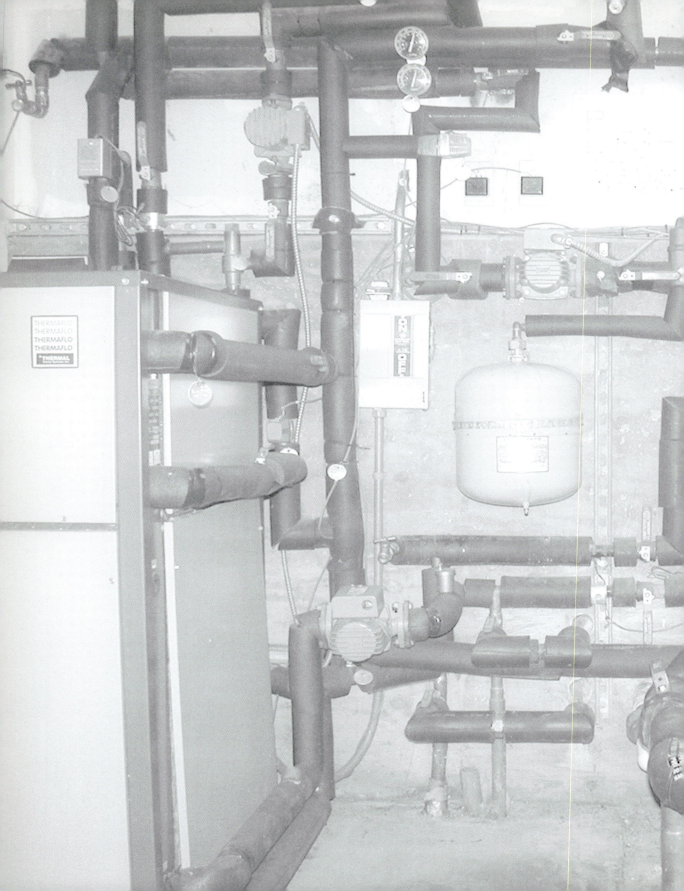

Space heating

7.1 SEASONAL HEAT DEMAND

The outside temperature was measured with a Davis Weather Monitor II at 30-minute intervals to determine the "heating degree days" for the months of January through June 1995. Using 18.3°C (65°F) as the reference temperature, the definition of "heating degree days" are the number of degrees the living space needs to be heated times the number of days heat is needed. This indication of heating was first devised 75 years ago and is still very popular today, although the actual weather tapes used in computer modeling, as discussed earlier, have supplanted it more and more. The temperature is that of ambient air and not of the inside living space. So this is a measure of how much heat is needed if there was absolutely no heat source inside the building and no solar heat came streaming in through the windows or was conducted out of the structure to the earth. It is based on the fact that heating in a building is not required when the outdoor average daily temperature is 18.3°C (65°F). The measured results of weather state from the on-site Davis Instrument

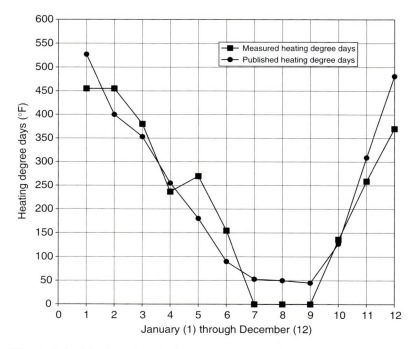

Figure 7.1   Heating degree days measured on-site.

are shown in Figure 7.1. Also for comparison are the standard tabulated results (Kreith and Kreider, 1978). These compare closely with those used in the Micropas Model used for energy management modeling and evaluation of the different building design concepts.

Now given this heat demand, one's choice is to select various heat sources, such as solar thermal, electric heat, gas heat, etc., to provide heating of the space up to the reference temperature of 18.3°C (65°F) and doing this in the most cost-effective, energy-saving, environmental conscious manner.

7.2   SOLAR THERMAL COLLECTOR HEAT UTILIZATION IN WINTER

The eight Heliodyne Gobi solar thermal collectors were used to provide 99% of the DHW needs and some weeks of radiant floor heating. There was still plenty of solar heating capacity to provide swimming pool temperatures within an acceptable range from 25°C (77°F) to 34.5°C (92°F) from early April to the end of October. As shown earlier, the extra heat, after all other heat demands were served, was dumped into the swimming pool. So how was the solar thermal heat being utilized throughout the year?

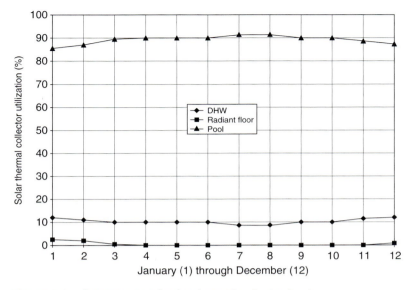

Figure 7.2   Percent use of solar thermal collector heat.

Figure 7.2 shows the fraction of pool, DHW, and building winter space heating demand that is supplied by solar thermal collector heat, via heat-pump radiant floor heat. About 90% of this collector heat is used for the pool, and then DHW and finally the radiant floor. This result was rather surprising, since it would be thought that there would be much more demand for radiant floor heating. But it was discovered that when it was cold, cloudy and rainy, requiring radiant floor heating, the solar thermal heat was not available.

It would be possible to store this solar collector heat in a large tank and then supply heat to the radiant floor from this stored heat during cold, cloudy weather. However, this capability is not incorporated into the design. The substantial heat loss that results from the DHW heat, storing sensible heat in hot water is not very efficient. Much more would have to be done, such as better insulation on the tanks, thermal isolation of the tank structural supports, and low thermal conductivity piping in and out of the heat storage tank.

Future solar homeowners may want to consider this option. There are solar houses that make large use of the hot water storage for space heating over long periods of cold weather. There is a solar home (commonly called the Haywood House) just outside of Portland, Maine. It has a very large basement with four water tanks about 2.4 m in diameter and 2.4 m tall (8 ft diam. × 8 ft tall) that supplied DHW and space heating. Clearly there must be a large portion of the house volume dedicated to these large tanks with their insulation. These and other concepts can be computer modeled and explored in performance and cost as discussed in Chapter 2 and the following chapters.

In view of the discussion above, other means of space heating are dominant in the Berkeley house. In addition to the solar thermal collector heat, there is building space heating supplied by greenhouse heat, solarium heat, and ground-source heat pump heat. These features require that the shape and orientation of the building envelope be carefully considered.

7.3   DESIGN OF BUILDING ENVELOPE

In earlier chapters we discussed the orientation and slope of the solar thermal collectors as well as the solar PV collectors. The 45° slope and the orientation just a little south west, required the large roof also to be sloped to 45°. This slope continued down as low as possible to include the greenhouse and solarium. This has been shown in Figures 1.5, 4.1 and 4.2. This configuration has been very practical and performs very well. The design was completed by Nold Residential Design (Nold, 1995).

The 45° slope over a large distance lends itself to a vaulted exposed beam ceiling as shown in Figure 7.3. Although this looks simple, there are a number of challenges that result from building code requirements. For example, on top of these huge beams there is a very thick (19 cm (7.5″)) stressed skin foam insulation roof panels of 3 m or 10 ft in width and interlocked by tongue and groove edges. Through these panels holes are cast for fire sprinkling piping and for electrical conduit for ceiling fans, sensors, etc. These prefabricated, polystyrene foam panels are manufactured by R-Control providing R-30 insulation and minimal infiltration, and fixed into the ceiling beams with large, long screws. The code required that these screws be tested with hydraulic jacks to assure they had the required strength. The beams were Para-Lams made from wood waste and owing to their method of manufacturing under high temperature and high pressure they are extremely strong without any knots or weak points as in normal, naturally grown wood. Consequently, the screws fix into this wood much stronger than in ordinary wood. Para-Lam beams are highly recommended and they can be made in almost any size and any length.

Another challenge was that the eaves had to be constructed in these foam roof panels, so that the foam was interrupted by fire-block break wood frame members, to prevent carrying the fire up into the roof during a fire storm. These details were required by the code and were based on fire testing in severe

Figure 7.3   Exposed beam ceiling inside of 45° slope roof.

firestorm conditions which are too common in forested, hilly areas of California.

The remaining portion of the building envelope was dictated by the living space requirement within the house and the shape of the lot rather than by the solar roof. The angular arrangement required to meet all these constraints was shown in Figure 4.2.

7.4   RADIANT FLOORS

A schematic cross section of the house showing the locations of each of the radiant floor coils in each of the rooms is shown in Figure 7.4. The air circulation ducting for heating and air conditioning, fireplace heating, and greenhouse heating is also shown. The radiant floor heating system used 480 m (1575 linear feet) of Wirsbo 15.8 mm (5/8") PEX tubing buried in a 38 mm (1.5") Gypcrete® over-pour on top of the structural slab of the lower floor and on top of the plywood sub-floor in the two upper living areas.

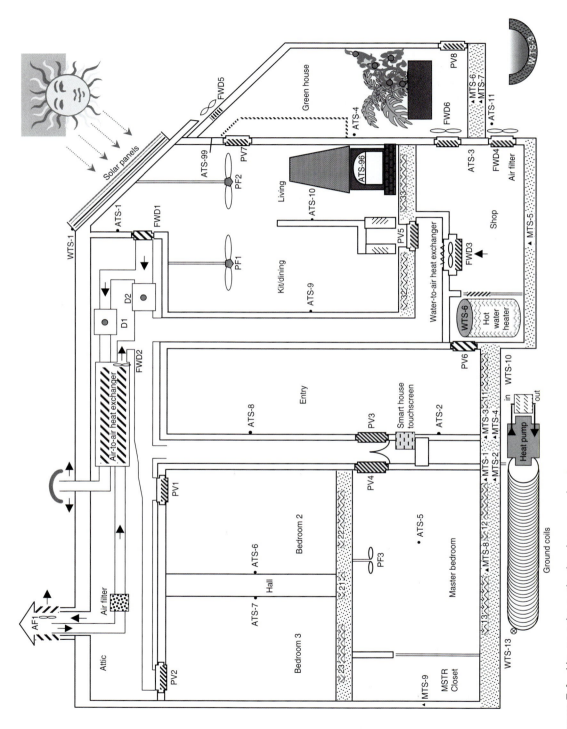

Figure 7.4   House schematic showing space heat sources.

Each of the living areas with radiant heating has its own temperature control so that the hot glycol is controlled through these zones to achieve the temperature set-point. The solar system piping and instrumentation diagram is shown in Figure 7.5, with each of the floor radiant coils shown.

There are two modes of operation of the radiant floor heating: (A) solar heat from roof collectors circulating hot glycol through the floor coils and (B) heated glycol from the heat pump circulated through the floor coils.

Mode A sends the hot glycol from the solar collectors at the upper left of this diagram, down through valve AV6 and up through valve AV5 into pump P3 that does the circulation. The return takes the cooled glycol back, via valve AV3, through HX to pump P2, and through AV2, to the solar collectors to accept more heat. In this mode the solar collectors are used only for radiant floor heating and cannot be used for swimming pool heating. Due to this restraint, this option is not being used now and two ball valves are closed off, disabling this mode, as shown in Figure 7.5.

In the second mode, B, the heat pump is used. There are three major items in this complex diagram that relate to the radiant floor: (1) Radiant floors at upper right, (2) Heat pump at lower left of center, and (3) Ground coils at bottom left. The way this system functions is that 15.6°C (60°F) glycol in the ground coils is circulated by pump P4 through the source-side heat exchanger of the heat pump. In this mode, valve AV5, left of the heat pump, is closed. The heat pump uses electric energy to operate the pump and circulate Freon in a thermodynamic cycle to heat the sink-side heat exchanger. The sink heat is transferred to the glycol to heat it to 46°C (115°F) to heat the radiant floor coils via pump P3. The cooled glycol from the floor is returned via AV3 (position B) to the heat pump for more heating. The heat pump, charged with Freon®22, supplied by Thermal Energy Systems (1992), was intentionally sized with a ⅛ hp motor at the minimum to reduce electrical peak load on the solar PV system. The specs were 14.3 kW (49 kBtu/hr) on heating and 11.4 kW (39 kBtu/hr) on cooling. The coefficient of performance (COP), was 3.8 and the energy efficiency ratio (EER) was 14.4. On testing, this heat pump will heat the whole house up to 20°C (68°F) overnight. It works very well.

In practice, it is the radiant floor heat-pump heating (Mode B) that is used when greenhouse heat and fireplace heat are no longer available. This is only during cloudy, cold weather or at night, when there is no sun available to heat the glycol. Mode B works very well and maintains a very even house temperature. The heat pump, with such a small motor, operates very quietly and cannot be heard throughout the living areas of the house.

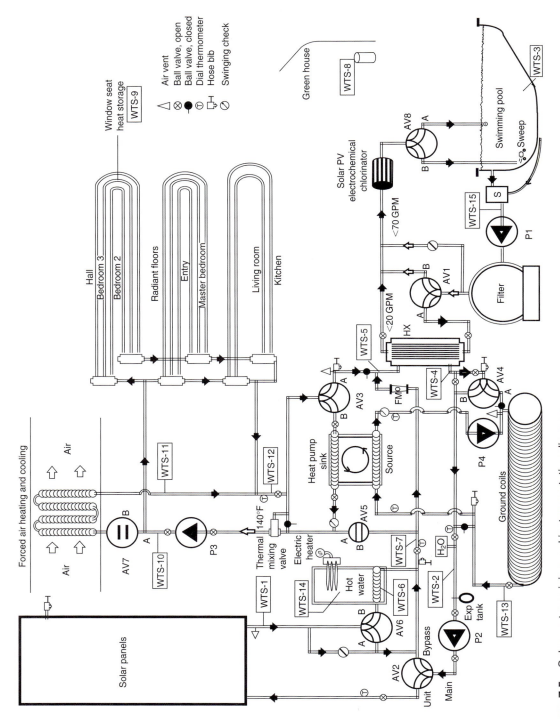

Figure 7.5   Solar system piping and instrumentation diagram.

Also in Mode B, the solar collector heating of the swimming pool is routinely done at the same time. The swimming pool piping loop takes heat from the solar panels through valve AV6 (position A), through the swimming pool heat exchanger, HX, and circulated through the solar PV powered electro-chemical chlorinator to the pool. The cooled glycol is then returned through the sand filter via a large pump, P1, and through valve AV1 (in position A) back to HX and circulated by pump, P2, back to the solar collectors via valve AV2 (in position "Unit") to be warmed again. When the sun is up during the day, all this equipment is completely powered by the solar PV collectors.

7.5   LIVING COMFORT

A warm radiant floor is something very special to experience. It is believed that a human body responds much better to their feet being warm than their head. In addition there is a warm radiation of low level of heat from the floor and one feels very comfortable at a lower temperature. This further lowers the cost of heating a house.

The radiant floor works under carpeting just as well as under a tiled floor. And, although it was not tried, it is believed to work well under a veneer hardwood floor as well. Since a simple valve easily controls the radiant coils, it only heats those rooms that require heat to reach their individual set-point. This is a further saving. Their operation is also absolutely silent and there is no air blowing noise or drafts felt, as with conventional HVAC (heating, ventilation, and air conditioning) systems. Radiant floors are certainly something very special to experience.

7.6   GEOTHERMAL HEAT PUMP AND LOCATION OF UNDERGROUND COILS

The concept of a "Geothermal heat pump" may be foreign to most readers, but it is widely used in the midwest in the US and in northern Scandinavian countries. See Geothermal Heat Pump Association (GHPA, 2003) for support and background. The key to this concept is that 1–2 m (3–6 ft) below ground surface, the temperature of the soil is around a steady 15.6°C (60°F), independent of summer or winter season. The heat pump operates like a refrigerator, with heat-dissipating coils at its back and coils inside for cooling. The refrigerator compressor circulates Freon® in both coils. In the coil inside of the refrigerator, the Freon® is expanded through an expansion valve and is boiled and vaporized in this coil, cooling the inside. This Freon® vapor is then compressed to a hot liquid and circulated to the coils in back of the refrigerator where it losses its heat and the cool Freon® liquid is returned to the expansion valve for removing more heat from the inside of the refrigerator. As this cycle continues, the inside of the refrigerator cools to very low temperatures by removing the residual heat and this unwanted heat is dumped in the back of the refrigerator in these heat loss coils.

The geothermal heat pump operates similarly – with one coil buried deep in the ground and the other one in the radiant floors. So the Freon® dumps its heat into a heat exchanger called "sink" which heats the glycol that runs through and heats the radiant floors. The other side of the heat pump has a heat exchanger called "source" which has ground temperature glycol circulating through it. So in this way heat from the ground is amplified by the heat pump and used to heat the radiant floor. In some places, this is called a "ground-source heat pump." The amplification of heat by the heat pump occurs because there is electric power running the compressor. So it is like using electric power to heat the floors, except that it is 3 or 4 times more efficient than using electric resistive heat. This big improvement factor over resistive heat is called the COP. A photograph of the Berkeley house heat pump is shown in Figure 7.6.

Another advantage of the geothermal heat pump is that it can be reversed. In this way, in the cooling cycle mode, the heat is removed from the house and dumped into the ground outside, where ground is 15.6°C (60°F), which is much cooler than the hot outside air temperature. However, the radiant floor cannot be used for cooling, since the cold floor sometimes condenses water out of the air and the tiles become slippery. If carpet is used, the condensed water moisture will rot the carpet. So the cooling coils are placed in the air ducting as in Figure 7.4 where the cool air is now circulated to each of the living spaces that demand cooling. These air-cooling coils are shown in the piping schematic in Figure 7.5 and are used with cooling mode when valve AV7 is opened. In cooling mode internal valves of the radiant floor coils are all closed and so they are not used.

Now it is evident why this geothermal heat pump system is found to be very efficient. In heating mode, it only has to boost the temperature of the ground at 15.6°C (60°F), up to say 46°C (115°F) to heat the floor, when the outside air temperature maybe 5°C (41°F) or colder. And in cooling air-conditioning mode, it can use the cool ground at 15.6°C (60°F) to cool the house coils to 10°C (50°F) which cools the circulating air via ducting when the outdoor temperature is hot, like 38°C (100°F).

Figure 7.6   Photograph of Berkeley house geothermal heat pump.

This is a great advance in technology that is not used very much because most home designers are unfamiliar about it. These heat pumps are known as water source heat pumps, ground-source heat pumps, or geothermal heat pumps, and are slowly being advertised.

Now that one knows how this geothermal heat pump system works, the ground coils can be studied in detail. In the Berkeley house design, 610 m (2000 linear feet) of buried ground coils that were made by HeatLink have been used, and they consist of 1″ cross-linked polyethylene with oxygen-diffusion barrier. Since the construction site involved extensive retaining walls with deep excavation, it was very simple to insert these coils of large 1 m (3 ft) loops down into the ground excavation, as shown in Figure 7.7. The excavation ditch was lined with felt for the water infiltration/drainage piping to prevent clay infiltration. In-between the outer layer of felt and the actual soil, the ground coils were located as shown in Figure 7.7. The space between the ground and the coils was then back-filled with special sand, and then topped off with pea gravel. On top of

Figure 7.7   Photograph showing installation of ground coils.

everything was placed topsoil for gardens. The sand was a special size distribution that held water moisture so that heat could be efficiently transferred at high thermal conductivity. The entire installation followed the procedures and materials recommended by the Geothermal Heat Pump Association (GHPA, 2003). The system in Figure 7.8 has worked very well for about 10 years and needed no maintenance.

For sites where no excavation is planned, deep wells have been used where the coils are inserted to achieve contact with the ground through ground water. There are also installations where the coils are laid down into a deep lake. See Geothermal Heat Pump Association (GHPA, 2003) for a background on different installations.

7.7   THERMAL ZONE CONTROLS

The thermal zone controls are a critical part of the larger solar system operation (Table 7.1). So if the heating mode is activated, then there are choices for delivery mode, delivery device, and energy source. The following section covers how these choices are made in the automatic control system (Figure 7.8).

The solar house is definitely a challenge to control since there are various sources of heat available and these must be used at the right time. The solar houses of the past usually required the occupant to make many decisions and required manual intervention, while some solar houses were built as an engineering experiment with huge quantities of thermal data pouring in to a large mainframe computer, requiring off-line analysis for control decisions. Today, energy control systems have advanced tremendously, are much more cost-effective, and now can be installed and maintained by large building control firms. The solar house resident interacts with the controller which is a color touch-screen and is very obvious to any member of the family. Inappropriate actions also are overridden by the control system, so now the system is fail-safe and idiot-proof as well. It is a new day for controlling the solar

Table 7.1   Thermal zone controls.

Functional mode	Delivery mode	Delivery device	Energy source
• Heating	• Heat pump	• Radiant floors	• Solar collector
• Cooling	• Heat pump	• Air duct	• Ground coils
• Hot water			• Swimming pool

Figure 7.8   Photograph showing the solar piping/control system.

house. The following will excite one with options for their own choosing.

The author's Berkeley house started out as a complex engineering experiment with 47 temperature sensors located everywhere, remote position indicators for valves and dampers with some 250 inputs to the computer. The computer logic was all invented from scratch and custom applied to the job. The computer language was C++ and had 250 pages of code of 50 lines per page. To change any control parameter a top-level software engineer and electronics engineer were required to make changes. Although it worked reliably for 8 years, it was clearly not the control system one would want in their house to manage. Then came the huge step forward to the modern age of energy management controllers.

The system running the house now is manufactured by Invensys with software by Tridium (Figure 7.8). This system is the newest and latest in the state-of-the-art. It was installed and is maintained under routine service contract by Yamas Controls out of their office in South San Francisco. Yamas Controls handle a large fraction of commercial buildings around the US, along with Honeywell, Johnson Controls and well known others. Yamas is a well-known and well-respected firm who has 40 years of experience in control systems. They handle many of the older and well-known controllers found in commercial buildings. So when they were asked to update the old control system, when a power spike killed the computer and destroyed the original software, they were delighted for the opportunity to do their first solar house and enter this needed market in a big way. Ones' solar house controls will be in excellent hands.

Here is how the system logic works for handling the various solar modes in this house. There are three sources of energy to heat the house living spaces in priority:

1. Greenhouse solar heat: If it is hot, its heat is sent to the house where it is needed.
2. Wood fireplace: If the fire is hot, its heat is distributed to the house where needed.
3. Heat pump-heated radiant floor: If neither of the above are possible the heat pump heats.

The house has 8 temperature control zones that can have different temperature set points. There are 12 temperature inputs and 8 damper position switches to read. It is much simpler. If cooling is required, it is determined by the living room temperature. Once this system is triggered into cooling mode, no other room can be heated simultaneously. This decision is appropriate for a single family house, since it avoids either the standard "reheat system" found in almost all commercial buildings or the individual room heat pump providing heating or cooling individually. This decision greatly reduces the piping complexity and equipment cost for a solar house. This is an important decision that should be reviewed by the owner/designer/contractor early in the solar house planning phase.

In parallel and independently to the above, solar energy provides DHW and heats the swimming pool. This decision gave DHW the highest priority for using solar collector heat, with the extra being sent to the pool. It can be noted that solar heat from the two sections of the greenhouse (fixed one and vented one) for space heating is entirely unaffected by solar demand for hot water or pool. This logic is shown in Table 7.2. Having two separate solar source control loops provided a major simplification possible to the control logic and uncoupled it from season-dependent control logic requirements. As a result this greatly reduced the cost. However, there is no better method than personally living in a solar house to optimize and tune the controls.

Table 7.2 Temperature control logic table.

DEVICE	Location	All off	Radiant H.P. heating	Greenhouse heating	Fireplace heating	H.P. air cooling	Nocturnal cooling	Greenhouse cooling
Macro=>> (conditional)		na	if ATS-10 < 65	if ATS-99 > ATS-10	if ATS-96 > 125	if ATS-11 > ATS-10 > 72°F	if ATS-11 < ATS-10	if ATS-4 > 115
			Heat ATS-10 to 65±1	Heat ATS-10 to 67±1	Heat house by fireplace	Cool ATS-10 to 72±1	Cool ATS-10 to 69±1	Cool ATS-4 to 100
Time period=>			24 hrs	24 hrs	24 hrs	24 hrs	6:15 pm–6:30 am	24 hrs
Touch screen		Away	Radiant floors	Greenhouse heat	Fireplace heat	Chilled air	Nocturnal cooling	Greenhouse cooling
Thermostat		off	Heating	off	off	Cooling	off	off
Heat pump		B	Heating	B	B	Cooling	B	B
AV3		off	Closed	Closed	Closed	Closed	Closed	Closed
AV5		off	Closed	Closed	Closed	Closed	Closed	Closed
AV7		off	Closed	Closed	Closed	**OPEN**	Closed	Closed
P3&4		off	**ON**	off	off	**ON**	off	off
D1		off	Closed	Closed	Closed	Closed	**OPEN**	Closed
D2		off	Closed	**OPEN**	**OPEN**	Closed	Closed	Closed
PF1		off	down if ATS-1 > ATS-9	down if ATS-1 > ATS-9	down if ATS-1 > ATS-9	off	up if ATS-1 > ATS-9	off
PF2		off	down if ATS-1 > ATS-9	down if ATS-1 > ATS-9	down if ATS-1 > ATS-9	off	up if ATS-1 > ATS-9	off
AF1		off	off	off	off	off	**ON** if ATS-11 < ATS-5 & nite	off
FWD1		off	off	**ON**	**ON**	off	off	off
FWD2		off	off	off	off	off	off	off
FWD3		off	off	off	off	off	**ON**	off
FWD4		off	off	off	off	**ON**	**ON**	off
FWD5		off	off	off	off	off	off	off
FWD6		off	off	**ON**	off	off	off	**ON**
PV1	BR2	Closed	Closed	Temp control ATS-6	Temp control ATS-6	Temp control ATS-6	Temp control ATS-6	na
PV2	BR3	Closed	Closed	Temp control ATS-7	Temp control ATS-7	Temp control ATS-7	Temp control ATS-7	na
PV3	Entry	Closed	Closed	Temp control ATS-2	Temp control ATS-2	Temp control ATS-2	Temp control ATS-2	na
PV4	MBR	Closed	Closed	Temp control ATS-5	Temp control ATS-5	Temp control ATS-5	Temp control ATS-5	na
PV5	Living	Closed	Closed	Temp control ATS-10	Temp control ATS-10	Temp control ATS-10	Temp control ATS-10	na
PV6	H.W. Room	Closed	Closed	Closed	Closed	Closed	Closed	Closed
PV7	Dining	Closed	Closed	**OPEN**	Closed	Closed	Closed	Closed
PV8	GRN House	Closed	Closed	Closed	Closed	Closed	Closed	**OPEN**
RH11	Entry	off	Temp control ATS-2	off	off	off	off	off
RH12	MBR east	off	Temp control ATS-5	off	off	off	off	off
RH13	MBR west	off	Temp control ATS-5	off	off	off	off	off
RH21	2nd Fl hall	off	Temp control ATS-8	off	off	off	off	off
RH22	BR2	off	Temp control ATS-6	off	off	off	off	off
RH23	BR3	off	Temp control ATS-7	off	off	off	off	off
RH32	Kit/dining	off	Temp control ATS-9	off	off	off	off	off
RH33	Living	off	Temp control ATS-10	off	off	off	off	off

Notes: Night – Night runs 6:15 pm–6:30 am; AF – Attic fan used at night 6:15 pm–6:30 am; AV – Automatic valve, two position, 2-Port: open or closed, or 3-Port: A or B position; P – Pump, single speed; D – Duct damper, open or closed; FWD – Fan with damper, two direction, variable speed option; PF – Ceiling paddle fan, two direction, three speed; PV – Panel vent damper, variable opening; RH – Radiant heat in floor; HP – Heat pump off if wts10 < 40 or >150 to protect compressor.

To accomplish the above, there are actively controlled 3 automatic valves, 2 small pumps, 2 ceiling paddle fans, 6 ducted fans, 8 control louver dampers, and 8 radiant floor loops with valves for a 2.5-bath/3-bedroom house with living room, dining room, kitchen, atrium entry, home office, library, greenhouse sitting area, and hallways – totaling 180 m^2 (1868 ft^2) of conditioned space. Other unconditioned space includes entry porch sunroom, family hobby shop area, wine cellar, and oversized double garage with wood shop area and pool equipment area, totaling 80 m^2 (832 ft^2) of unconditioned space.

For the solar house resident, the wall-mounted 15" color touch screen is the focal point. It is kept at adult height so that children cannot reach it. Even if they did, nothing serious can happen, since critical functions are multiple control key and/or password protected. It has multiple pages displaying a diagram of the house with displayed temperatures and active graphics showing which modes are operative at the moment, vents open, fans on, radiant coils heated, etc., with floor plans, logic diagram, etc. This screen could be placed around the house at different locations, though it was not necessary in the case of Berkeley house.

From this touch screen, local temperature set-points can be changed, modes can be over-ridden, and schedule changed on hourly, weekly, or monthly basis. To change any control parameters two areas must be touched in proper sequence, further reducing operation by the uninitiated. The system has multiple password barriers and an oversight advisory that prevents any action in changing controls that could result in unacceptable or un-safe operations.

The main controller is called "JACE," and it has a battery backup and many password security levels preventing unauthorized access to the control software code stored in its ram memory. It measures the size of a standard textbook and is sent signals from remote controllers that read temperatures, valve positions, etc. The remote controllers are small and of the size of two slices of bread stacked together and linked by a simple twisted pair of wire using a new internationally-accepted Lontalk® control protocol. This allows for the small controllers to be located up to 150 m (500 ft) away in a location nearer to the source of its input. They can be daisy-chained together very simply in a house. This avoids the need for a control closet to house all centralized equipment with all wiring home-run into this closet. The remote controllers can be mounted in the wall in a small electrical box with a flush cover. So this is a huge step toward miniaturization and greatly simplifies space in the house, installation complexity and cost.

The programming is very simple for the "control techs," who can "bind" any of the control devices to the control logic by just using graphic images ("plug & play") and control boxes. This avoids writing software completely and debugging and the errors that can result. In addition, the documentation is on-line and available in any detail desired.

A schematic cross section of the house showing the locations of each of the living space temperature control zones has been presented in Figure 7.4. In the Berkeley house there are eight temperature control zones with individual temperature set-points. For the radiant floor coils, there are eight radiant floor coil valves, RH11 through RH33, where the first digit refers to the house floor number and the second to the valve. For the cooling air conditioning, there are eight motorized vents that regulate the cooling air flow into the individual temperature zones, PV1 through PV8. The control logic table is shown in Table 7.2.

Across the top of this table are each of the control modes: all off, radiant heat pump heating, greenhouse heating, fireplace heating, heat pump air cooling, nocturnal cooling, and greenhouse cooling. Under each of these modes is the control logic conditional that tells the control system which temperatures to examine, which to compare, and what to do. Down the left side are all the control devices, such as valves, pumps, dampers, ceiling paddle fans, attic fan, duct fans, motorized vents, and radiant coil valves. Throughout the center of this table are the actions that are carried out. As discussed earlier, all of this logic in entered in non-volatile random access memory in the JACE controller (Invensys, 2003) that has battery backup. The control logic is accomplished with graphics by selecting and moving the appropriate control boxes around on the screen and linking the devices and setting the control functions and modes all graphically. This graphical interface then, actually writes the detail code that accomplishes the actions. So this makes the programming very much easier and transparent to the user. The homeowner may undertake the large task of doing this either by themselves or by a commercial control company hired under contract to do this as well as maintain the system under a 24-hour call response service. Having learned to do elementary logic programming, there is a steep learning curve to get efficient at it and keep refreshed so that the skill does not become stale. It is recommended that such a task be undertaken by professionals and a service contract.

To illustrate how the strategy of thermal controls work for a multi-mode, multi-zone control solar house, it should be illustrated how the system works as the temperature steadily increases from a very cold winter night. To start with a cold winter night, while one is reading a nice book by the crackling fire in the heat-producing fireplace, the ceiling paddle fans stirring the air very slowly in the living room, so that the fire-place heat is uniformly dispersed everywhere. The warm air at the peak of the roof is pulled by a small fan and sent to the individual living spaces (like bedrooms at this time) that are being warmed. By the time the last person is ready for bed, the fireplace (fire if safely behind a sealed, clear ceramic door) is left to die down and eventually cool. The living room temperature, ATS-10, is monitored and when it falls below 18.3°C (65°F), the radiant floor heat pump is turned on. As the house begins to cool slowly during the early morning hours, the lower temperature set-points of the individual rooms will be triggered and the radiant floor heat pump heating begins. This is silent and does not create any detectible sound – just a low, warm heat from the floor.

The temperature control logic accomplishing this is listed in the third column headed "Radiant H.P. heating" of Table 7.2. At the top it shows that ATS-10 is being checked against the mode set-point of 18.3°C (65°F) to turn on the heat pump. Along this column, one can see that the thermostats and the heat pumps are in heating mode and glycol pumps P3 and P4 are working to send the fluid from the sink and source sides of the heat pump to coils in the ground and in the floors. Further down this column, the two ceiling paddle fans, PF1 and PF2 are in action so that the air is pushed down to the center of the room and then up to the walls. The reason for this airflow direction will be explained in Section 7.9.

In the morning, the house is warm and uniform in temperature, and the tiles, carpet, or hardwood floors are warm for the feet. After breakfast, the sun begins to come up and the first rays hit the greenhouse and begin heating its plants and air inside. Now look at the fourth column, headed: "Greenhouse heating". When the greenhouse temperature, ATS-99, warms above the living room temperature, ATS-10, the radiant floor heating is turned off and the greenhouse vent is opened into the dining room and the greenhouse fan comes on low. This now takes the air from the lowest floor and moves it through the warm greenhouse and releases into the dining room. The paddle fans continue to turn in the same direction to maintain a uniform temperature as the space is further heated. The warm air that is up at the peak of the roof is sent via fan FWD1 to the individual rooms as their individual temperature sensors trigger. This warm air is controlled by variable vents, PV1 through PV8, as shown in this column. When any of these rooms reach their set-point temperature, their individual vents are closed off. When the living room reaches 20°C (68°F), then this greenhouse heating mode is complete. If the temperature in the living room, ATS-10, drops below 18.9°C (66°F), the greenhouse heating mode again

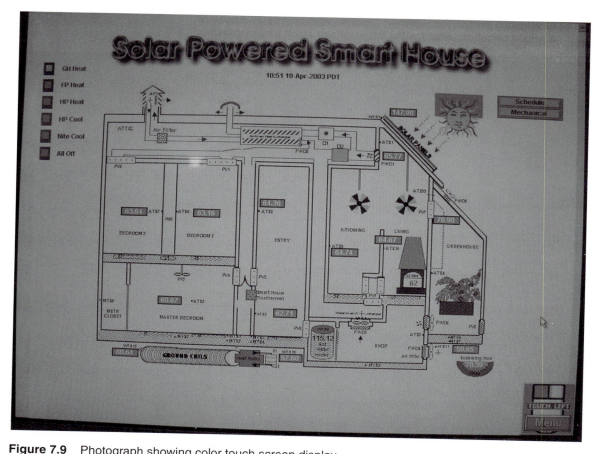

Figure 7.9   Photograph showing color touch screen display.

comes on, providing heat and raising the temperature to 68°F. There is a dead-band of ±1°F in the logic to prevent short cycling between the modes.

Putting the thermal zone controls altogether, Figures 7.9 and 7.10 shows the color-touch screen display and the surface wall mount. This allows the display of temperature in each zone and which modes are operating at any given time as shown in the upper left portion of the screen. When the sun is out and the solar collectors are using heat, the graphic of the sun appears. At the upper right, there are also hot buttons to pull up the scheduling block to change when certain modes come on or off. There is another hot button which will display the mechanical system diagram, shown in Figure 7.5. This is a most useful screen for displaying and allowing local control of any mode set-point, any living zone temperature, as well as the amount of hot water storage, the swimming pool temperature and the temperature of the ground coils.

Figure 7.10 Photograph showing color touch screen wall mount.

This control system is web-based, which means that under maintenance contract (with Yamas Control), outside service people can dial into the system, display the graphic page of the status, and change the software if needed. This also allows the homeowner to dial in and examine the status or change any of the control set-points. With the availability of wireless personal digital assistant (PDAs such as Palmtops), the homeowner can dial into this control system from anywhere within the house and check the status or change the set-points.

The installation is very cost-effective with an installation cost of US $26,950. Figure 7.11 shows the individual control modules mounted inside the control closet, the door for which is shown on the right side of Figure 7.10. These Invensys controllers measure the temperatures throughout the house, positions of valves, dampers, etc. and are linked via a Lontalk® net to the main JACE controller at the left. There is a drawer-mounted laptop below that allows for local programming and enables the graphic display, color touch screen.

Figure 7.11   Photograph showing control closet hardware.

7.8   WOOD FIREPLACE BACKUP HEAT

Figure 7.12 shows the heat-producing fireplace (manufactured by Regency, 1995). The ceiling paddle fans are turned on, stirring the air very slowly in the living room so the fireplace heat is uniformly dispersed everywhere. The warm air at the peak of the roof is pulled out by a small fan and sent to the individual living spaces (like bedrooms in the above scenario) that are being warmed.

The fireplace has a small fan built inside that pulls in room air below the hearth and passes it through high alloy tubes radiantly heated by the fire. The heated air is exhausted through the vent just above the hearth and below the decorative hood. This warm air is directed to anyone sitting in front of the fire to quickly warm them. Also there is substantial radiation from the fire transmitted through the clear ceramic glass in the door panel that further warms people in front of the fireplace.

Figure 7.12   Photograph showing heat-producing fireplace.

The small fan comes on automatically when the fireplace hearth rises above 74°C (165°F) and turns off when it falls below 40°C (107°F). In addition to this built-in bi-metal temperature sensor, the same region of the hearth is fitted with a thermistor to also send the measured temperature to the house automatic control system. This thermistor allowed the control system to detect the fireplace heat and to switch off heat pump heating or greenhouse heating, and transfer into the fireplace heating mode. This fireplace heating system worked very well and was a wonderful warm experience for anyone sitting in front of the crackling fire reading a book or magazine.

7.9   CEILING FANS IN WALL UPFLOW

The two ceiling paddle fans, PF1 and PF2 are installed so that the air is pushed down to the center of the room and then up to the walls as in Figure 7.3. This air moving up at the walls, tends to restrain any heavier colder air, naturally convecting downward, from colder outside walls of the house. This action is like providing extra insulation against the colder walls and improving the heat efficiency of the house.

The slow air circulation also further insures that there are no pockets of hot air gathering up in the high vaulted ceiling beam areas or down at the floor level where people are sitting. The air circulation rate should be so low that people will not feel a breeze. There is clearly an optimum circulation rate. Ceiling paddle fans have three speeds forward and reverse and this system can be used to select the correct air flow direction and its strength. The paddle fan controls installed in the Berkeley house allowed for any of the three speeds to be employed by the control system, but in practice the medium speed was about optimum for the geometry of the house. Two fans were required to cover the whole area of the living room and kitchen/dining area to insure good air mixing, without excessive breeze.

The use of such slowly turning ceiling fans located high up in the vaulted ceiling, corrects one of the problems many people did not like about solar houses with large, steeply sloped roofs, optimized for solar collectors. They felt the large, dark cavernous area made the living space difficult to heat and seemed cold. These fans corrected the temperature stratification of such large vaulted ceiling spaces.

7.10   AMBIANCE

Proper lighting can correct the second criticism of the large, dark cavernous area of the sloped solar roof. So finally to complete the effect of creating a pleasant ambiance to the living room, kitchen and dining areas, there was soffit lighting that provided a wash of light up into the massive roof beam

Figure 7.13   Photograph showing soffit lighting of ceiling rafters.

area as in Figure 7.13. This soffit lighting also had a small down-directed wash of light along the room walls to reduce the contrast from ceiling to walls. In this way, there was a soft light emanating from the ceiling area. This lighting was dimmable and in three sections, so the right ambiance of lighting could be selected to create the proper mood most appropriate for whatever event was underway in any of the living spaces. Figure 7.13 shows a view of soffit lighting for one of the mood settings from such lighting.

Figure 7.14   Photograph of entry sunroom.

Another ambiance feature in a solar design is a solar-heated entry sunroom as shown in Figure 7.14. This entry sunroom provides an excellent place for visitors to be greeted without having to stand in the outside inclement weather. It also provides a space out of the rain where packages can be left by delivery services without damage. Also important is that

Figure 7.15   Photograph showing a place to sit in the entry sunroom.

packages containing food items left inside this space are no longer a tempting treat for hungry Rancoons!

Inside this entry sunroom, there is a great space to sit and have coffee and read the morning newspaper or magazine, as shown in Figure 7.15. It is highly recommended that such a solar feature be incorporated in one's solar design.

8

Space cooling

8.1   COOLING RADIANT FLOORS IS NOT RECOMMENDED

It is important to first express a conclusion about space cooling. The radiant floor cannot be used for cooling since the cold floor sometimes condenses water from the air and the tiles become slippery. Condensation occurs when the floor surface temperature falls below the dew point of the house air. The floor is comparable to a cold drink when condensation occurs on the glass surface from the humidity in the air. Extensive testing over a range of typical house conditions for different types of weather conditions outside, derived that in almost all situations, as soon as the floor became noticeably cool, condensation was detected making the floor slippery. Further, if carpet is used, the condensed water moisture will rot the carpet. So we do not recommend cooling the radiant floors.

8.2   NOCTURNAL COOLING STRATEGY

Another inexpensive solar house design feature that is very impressive and successful is the function of "nocturnal cooling." This is also called "free cooling" since it is not always at night. It works in all climates with colder outside temperatures and lower humidity. It is very simple in concept. When the outside temperature falls below the inside temperature and the house needs cooling, then a large louver vent located near the shady north-side of the house is opened to let in the cool outside air. Simultaneously, a similar sized vent is opened in the ceiling or high in a wall in the warmest location of the house.

Large motor-operated dampers are inexpensive and widely available (i.e. Grainger). This creates a strong natural convection circulation bringing in the cooler, denser air to the lower levels of the house and exhausting the warmer lower density air at the higher levels. This density difference drives this natural convection circulation very well and no energy-consuming fans are needed when the vent areas are large enough (i.e. $1\,m^2$ or $10\,ft^2$), like window-size openings. Assisting fans can be used (i.e. 30–100 m^3/min or 1000–3000 cfm) if no large area can be planned or located, but even small fans of 1/8–1/4 hp can add about 50–100 kWh/month to the electricity consumption since they operate most of the evening. A good planning and design will contribute to huge savings. In addition, small, slowly operating paddle fans in the ceiling also helped the heat transfer at the ceiling, walls, and floor to make this nocturnal cooling even more efficient.

Many studies show that this needed cool air can be obtained by drawing warmer night-time outside air through a cold bed of rocks under the house and ground-coupled to keep them cool. This works in climates that do not cool significantly at night. Some fans may be needed to assist drawing the air through a bed of rocks that provide significant pressure drops, but if the rocks are 40 mm or 1.5-inch size and arranged with a large flow area, some amount of fan energy is needed. The rocks need to thermally conduct their warmth into the ground when not in use, otherwise the rock bed will become too warm to offer cooling relief for night-after-night use.

Another excellent cooling option is to bury 25–50 mm (1–2 inches) of large diameter plastic tubing in the ground around the house through which outside air can be pulled to obtain cooling. Many parallel runs are needed to be able to keep the dia-meter low enough so the tubing can be bent and to keep the pressure drop low. So if excavation is being done for foundations anyway, this design can be very attractive and worth considering. In a later chapter in this book, we will discuss ground-coupled tubing of small diameter with glycol fluid circulated to obtain cooling through a variable speed heat pump that air-conditions the house. The latter will be preferred in most climates and will be smaller and inexpensive to install.

The strategy of nocturnal cooling is to simply bring in cool air at night at a low point in the building and exhausting the

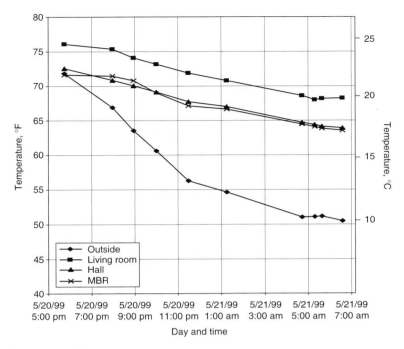

Figure 8.1   Nocturnal cooling in natural draft convection.

hot air out of the building at the highest point. This could be done by utilizing the natural convection-driven "chimney effect" which makes use of the fact that the cold air coming in is more dense and the hot air leaving is hot and less dense. This density difference causes the cold air to be pulled in and the hot air to leave at the highest point. When there is a fairly large outside-inside temperature difference of 5°C (9°F), the cooling works very well even without any fans. When nocturnal cooling mode is triggered by house temperatures over 20.6°C (69°F), the control system opens a large louvered vent at the lowest point on the cool north-side of the house and the attic damper vent opens to exhaust the hot air. Figure 8.1 shows the performance of such an operation.

When the temperature difference is very small, as it is in late summer and warm nights, this nocturnal cooling is improved by using fans. For this purpose, the house is fitted with an attic fan with variable speed that pulls the air out of the house. In the summer time, when nocturnal cooling mode is triggered by house temperatures over 20.6°C (69°F), the control system opens the large louvered vent at the lowest point on the cool north-side of the house and the damper vent is opened and the attic fan is operated. This pulls in the cool air much faster than would be possible in summertime. Figure 8.2 shows the performance of this operation.

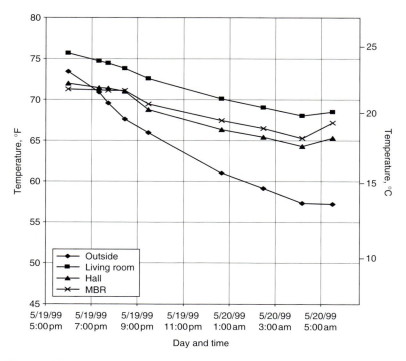

Figure 8.2   Nocturnal cooling in forced draft convection.

To conclude, nocturnal cooling will not work when the outside temperature is above the inside temperature. The advantage of the automatic controls is that during night, when the outside temperature drops below the inside temperature, nocturnal cooling is automatically initiated without any intervention from the occupants.

Another advantage of nocturnal cooling is that cool air is brought into the basement area, with massive amounts of concrete, to store the cold. So when heat pump cooling is needed, the cool air used for the HVAC distribution is taken from this cool basement area, further cooled by the heat pump and then distributed throughout the house as required by the thermal zones. This ducting arrangement can be seen in Figure 7.4. So it is good to include in the house design, a cold basement wherever possible as a source of cool air.

The air filtration of the cool air being pulled into the house could become a serious problem when there is street dust, debris from building constructions, smoke, etc. The standard building duct filter which is a pleated paper filter works well but requires a small booster fan, if the filter is thick, to remove the smaller particle sizes. If there are individuals in the house with allergies, asthma or respiratory conditions, this higher efficiency filter and booster fan ought to be considered. If there were a large wall area and vent, then the larger area will allow for a larger size filter, with less pressure drop and perhaps the booster fan would not be needed. For such considerations, the HVAC mechanical contractor should be consulted for sizing this filter and determining if a booster fan is needed.

8.3   PV-POWERED ATTIC FAN IS ONLY A PART-SOLUTION

There are many companies that offer a solar PV-powered attic fan. This sounds great and works during the day when the sun is up and the outside air is cooler than inside. But on a hot day with the outside air temperature well above the inside temperature, the last thing one would want to do is to pull in hotter outside air into a cooler house. If the attic was sealed from the house below and the fan pulled in air into the attic through vents at the eaves, the solar PV-powered attic fan would keep the attic cooler than without a fan, but would not cool the house itself significantly.

Further, when the outside air temperature drops below the house temperature at night-time, the attic fan pulls in cooler air from outside. Since solar power is not available at night, the large solar PV electric supply for the whole house works by reversing the meter under a net-metering program during daytime and just use grid power at night to run the house, including the attic fan on normal power. The total result of this approach to cooling the house at night is by using solar electricity credit accumulated during the daytime for use at night.

8.4   CEILING FANS IN WALL DOWNFLOW

The use of ceiling fans in helping the solar heating of the house was discussed in Section 7.9. Now for cooling the house these ceiling fans need to reverse and operate so that air flows up into the center of the fan and then blows down along the outside walls.

The purpose of this fan reversal is to hinder the warm layer of air rising upward by natural convection from the warmer outside walls. This wall downflow helps reduce the heat leakage from the hot outside air into the house, and it is worth the effort in getting the fan direction right.

Also when the house is warm, the very slow circulation of air makes people feel cooler and more tolerable of a slightly warmer inside temperature with the same degree of comfort.

8.5   GEOTHERMAL HEAT PUMP COOLING OF ROOM AIR

In summer, heat is rejected either to the pool or to the ground coils to cool the house. If the pool is too hot, the ground coils are used. Using the pool's natural cooling of 1°C (2°F) overnight on a typical summer day, calculations show a potential of 4 kW (333,600 Btu/day) could be rejected. Using a 1.3 divisor for the heat pump, it is expected to be able to transfer 3.1 kW (256,000 Btu/day) from the house into the pool. Micropas predicted a worst-case of cooling load of 4.7 kW (386,000 Btu/day) on August 20th; however the model did not include the beneficial effects of the Heat Mirror glazing, which was added after the computer modeling was done.

In the operation of heat pumps for cooling, the swimming pool provides a very attractive heat sink when air conditioning the house. By conditioning the house for about a week (the longest period of needed air conditioning during testing), the pool water temperature was increased by only 10°C (18°F). Maintaining the pool at pleasant summer swimming temperatures of up to 33.3°C (92°F) was easy with the bubble blanket cover pulled off at night. If there is a swimming pool in the solar house plan, then this pool heat pump mode is most attractive.

To demonstrate this pool mode, a test was performed that used the heat pump for cooling of the forced air circulation system, while rejecting heat to the pool. The flow rate of pool water through the plate heat exchanger was 45 L/min (12 gpm) with a ΔT of 1.4°C (2.5°F). The heat flux exchanged was determined as 4.4 kW (15,000 Btu/hr) on the pool side. On the heat pump cooling side, the flow rate of glycol was 21.8 L/min (5.75 gpm) with a ΔT of 1.9°C (3.5°F) to achieve a heat flux exchange of 3.5 kW (12,000 Btu/hr). The cool air exhausting the ducting was a steady 22.7°C (72.8°F).

The ground coil test using the heat pump to cool the house air was done on a 37.8°C (100°F) day on June 25, 1995. Figure 8.3 shows the outside temperature and the indoor performance of the house in 100°F weather. Glycol was pumped from the heat pump source side through the ground coils at 19.3 L/min (5.1 gpm) and demonstrated typically a 4.4°C (8°F) ΔT. This temperature history is also shown in Figure 8.3 and is discussed in Section 8.6. At the end of the first day, the heat pump was rejecting heat at 25°C (77°F) to the ground coils, with the coil returning cooler glycol at 31.1°C (82°F). This heat pump system cooled the house from 28.3°C to 25.6°C (83°F to 78°F) as shown in Figure 8.3.

During this test, in addition to supplying 7.2°C (45°F) cold glycol to the chilling heat exchanger in the forced air duct system circulating air to the first floor of the house, cold glycol was also supplied to the radiant floor sections in the

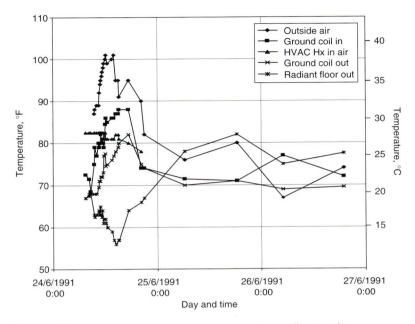

Figure 8.3   Ground coil temperature history in cooling mode.

tiled entry hall and the carpeted master bedroom. As shown in Figure 8.3, the radiant floor coils returned glycol initially 21.7°C (71°F) and declined to 13.3°C (56°F) by the end of June 25, by which time some weak effects of condensation, below the 16.1°C (61°F) dew point, were observed on few of the coldest tiles. The cool tiled floor gave the home occupants a significant positive cooling effect whereas the effect in the carpeted sections was not felt. The radiant floor coils equilibrated to near air temperature within 12 hours. However, the condensation problems were serious enough that this floor-cooling mode was abandoned.

It is recommended that the ground-coupled heat pump cooling of the air be considered. Despite these positive results with air-cooling, in protracted hot weather it is required to show that the ground coils can function effectively day-after-day in cooling mode. However, these long extended hot periods have not occurred till date. If such a condition prevails, when the ground coil exit temperature exceeds the maximum-allowed pool temperature (i.e. 32.2°C or 90°F), then the ground coils can be used concurrently rejecting heat to the pool.

8.6   THERMAL TRANSIENT/CAPACITY OF GROUND COILS

One of the important issues in using ground coils for the source side of the heat pump in cooling mode is the transient thermal behavior and their capacity for handling long-lasting cooling loads.

The transient behavior of these coils has been shown in Figure 8.3. The ground coils delivered cool glycol from 19.4°C to 27.8°C (67°F to 82°F) to the heat pump source side on the first day (June 25) as shown. And the ground coils recovered within 11 hours for additional cooling, shown in Figure 8.3 as "ground coil out" (diamond data symbols) temperatures recovered from 27.8°C (82°F) at 6 pm on June 25th down to 21.1°C (70°F) at 5 am June 26th. The next day (June 27th) with outside temperatures that peaked at 29.4°C (85°F), showed the ground coils to have dropped exponentially to around 20°C (68°F) after an additional 24 hours, but this is not significant for its additional cooling capacity.

Throughout the entire period of these three days, the house temperature was maintained at a pleasant 25°C (77°F), which seemed quite cool especially with the ceiling paddle fans operating in their medium speed mode.

In the years of experience after this initial testing the ground coils typically supplied cool glycol from 19.4°C to 23.3°C (67°F to 74°F) after a typical hot day. The chilled glycol out of the heat pump going to the air coils went down to about 4°C (39°F). Lowering the set-point below this point resulted in the low pressure overload breaker getting tripped. So operation of the ground-source heat pump requires some care and control tuning to get it right. It is believed that these operating characteristics will depend on the manufacture and model of the heat pump used. A professional HVAC supplier and installer would be recommended.

8.7   THERMAL ZONE CONTROLS

The thermal zone controls for the cooling mode are completely analogous to those for the heating modes discussed in Chapter 7 except for the following modes:

1. Heat pump air cooling
2. Nocturnal cooling
3. Greenhouse cooling.

The heat pump air cooling and the nocturnal cooling modes provide space cooling for thermal zones: bedroom 2, bedroom 3, entry hall, master bedroom, and living room. The cooling is supplied by chilled air entering each of the thermal zones through motorized vents in each space. The vent ducting is shown schematically in Figure 7.4. The cool air enters each of the rooms up at the ceiling via directed vent louvers and the warm air returns down into the cool basement where

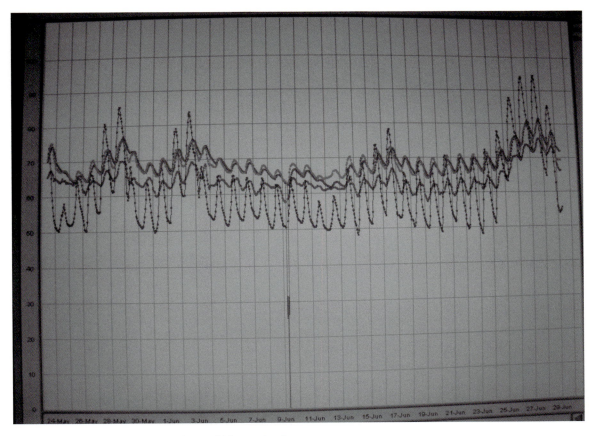

Figure 8.4   Display of house thermal history for June.

the air is further chilled by the heat pump chilled-heat exchanger in the air duct. This is very conventional except that it was preferable to have the chilled air forced into the room up at the ceiling. This provided additional mixing and prevented the thermal stratification that is so typical of chilled air space cooling designs.

The heat pump air cooling mode combined with nocturnal (free) cooling worked very well in automatic control covering a range of thermal zones of the house. Figure 8.4 shows the house performance over the month of June, ranging from night time cold air at 9.4°C (49°F) interrupted by a period of hot weather with peak temperatures up to 35.6°C (96°F). The living space was maintained around 20°C (68°F) throughout most of the month. As required by the automatic controls, nocturnal (free) cooling occurred during daytimes when the outside temperature was cooler than inside. On the very hot days, nocturnal (free) cooling started and did all that it could do before the outside temperature became too hot, and then

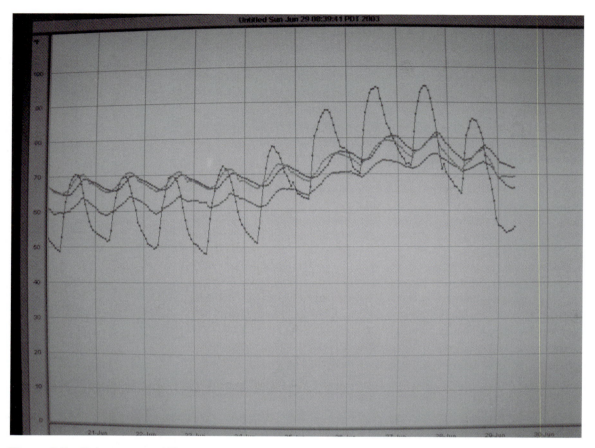

Figure 8.5   Enlargement of Figure 8.4.

automatically the heat pump air cooling took over to keep the living spaces mostly below 25.6°C (78°F), as shown in the enlarged section in Figure 8.5.

Figure 8.5 shows very well that during the cold foggy days the greenhouse heating was sufficient and only occasionally the heat pump heating was used to maintain the living space around 20°C (68°F). Then to the right of Figure 8.5 the living space temperatures were kept well below the hot outside air temperatures. The net result of using two cooling modes and two heating modes, the living space temperatures were maintained very well over extreme period of cold and hot days.

The third mode is greenhouse cooling which is for plant protection and has no significant impact on living spaces inside the house. This mode is triggered when the air in the upper region of the greenhouse reaches a temperature, ATS-99, of 48.9°C (120°F). At this point, a vent is opened at the top of the greenhouse that allows the hot air to leave, while the outside cool air enters through a large motorized vent at the bottom of the greenhouse. This natural convection venting occurs until the temperature drops to 38°C (100°F).

During hot summer times automatic temperature-controlled glass roof shades can be pulled to eliminate the hot sun. These shades can also be inside, but they function more effectively in keeping out the unwanted heat if they are located outside and on top of the glass roof. The author has not yet located cost-effective automatic shades of this type, but the designer may want to keep this option in mind. Actively controlled, movable louvers appear to be an attractive concept to be explored. They must be strong enough to tolerate large and gusty wind velocities.

It is advantageous to have a large thermal mass of soil in the planter boxes and in the brick or tiled concrete floor below them for carrying warm daytime temperatures into dark evening hours. It was found that massive amounts of soil were more space-efficient in holding sensible heat capacity than water drums. In addition, broad-spectrum solar lamps (i.e. Gro-lux) on timers helped extend the growing season during these early evening hours, greatly extending vegetables into winter.

The temperature gradients that can occur with vertical stratification were fully explored to understand what temperature extremes greenhouse plants might experience. It was found that a 15°C (25°F) temperature gradient is typical, so that placing plants in raised beds at mid-height, as shown in Figure 4.7, works very well. Most useful vegetable plants do not tolerate temperatures over 51°C (125°F), so design features and active temperature control becomes critical. Another fascinating result was that vegetables raised from seeds in this temperature environment did much better than vegetable plants brought in as fully-formed but small-sized plants. There seems to be a conditioning process at work here that gives seedlings a chance to adapt and grow productively in this environment. Automatic 15-minute drip watering and light spray in early morning and early evening worked best. Chicken manure worked much better than steer manure. Fresh salads every day for most of the year are a tremendous side-benefit of the solar greenhouse. A range of vegetables found to be successful and prolific throughout most of the year included chard, celery, lettuce of all varieties resistant to bolting, collards, tomatoes, beans, carrots, spices, and herbs. The solar homeowner can also enjoy trying more plant varieties.

PV electric power

9.1   GRID-CONNECTED, NET-METERING, AND TIME-OF-USE PRICING

Mounted on the 45° sloped roof just below the solar thermal collectors, there are six ASE-300 PV collectors (made by ASE Americas at Billerica, MA, now RWE Schott Solar, Inc.) mounted about 50 mm (2″) above the concrete-tiled roof. They are silicon-based and completely sealed between glass plates for long life. In California, they are qualified for a Class-A fire rating that is required in the wildlands fire risk area of the Berkeley and Oakland hills. An array of six PV collectors produces about 260 V DC that is fed into a Trace Engineering (now Xantrex) grid-tied inverter, Model SW4048UPV, that converts the DC power into 240 AC power to power the electrical system of the house. This system qualifies for the new "Net-metering" laws that permit the excess power that leaves the house to help support the local grid. The utility's analog power meter runs backward during this excess power period during every sunny day. When the sun is not shining, the power meter runs forward measuring the electrical power consumed by the house. The net difference at the end of the calendar year becomes the basis for billing (if any) at the standard electrical rate structure for a single family dwelling, which is currently 13¢/kWh. (One US cent is about €1.06 cents at the present exchange rates.) So after a whole year of power consumption of all the electrical equipment in the house, the electricity cost totals US $268 for the year and $296.78 with all taxes and fees included! To add, California electricity rates are some of the highest in the Nation.

The solar PV electric system operated flawlessly from the moment it was switched on. No maintenance had been required. The California utilities require a large AC disconnect switch (clearly labeled "Solar PV Disconnect") to be located outside the house near the main disconnect and the power meter, to enable the utility to manually open whenever a power line repair is needed. So grid-connected, net-metering PV systems are a success and the number of installations are increasing rapidly around the US and in Europe.

The newest added improvement on grid-tied, net-metering is "time-of-use (TOU) pricing." The goal of TOU pricing is to provide a significant incentive for solar PV systems to increase their production of electricity to augment the grid during the "peak hours" in trade for increased use of electricity "off peak." The critical times for "on-peak" are noon to 6 pm for the months of May through October, excluding weekends. This was selected because during these times and summer months, the air conditioning load in the hotter regions represents a huge demand on the local utilities, often requiring the use of expensive peaking power through turbo-generators, etc. "Off-peak" are the times outside of this period.

The net electrical power usage for the Berkeley house over an entire year and for each hour of the day has been shown in Table 9.1. In the upper portion of the table are the electrical consumption loads by type of load, the solar PV electricity produced, and the bottom portion shows the total loads and solar PV electricity for every hour. This table details the energy that is consumed (net) after the electricity produced from solar PV is subtracted by the net-metering function. For comparison, the solar PV electricity produced from the PV collectors averaged about 7.2 kWh/day on a sunny day.

Referring to Table 9.1, it should be noted that the breakdown of the electrical loads by each appliance, motor, or control is very helpful in revealing where the largest loads appear. For example, in the active solar systems where pumps are used to capture heat from the solar thermal panels, the glycol circulation pump is only 48 W and the flow rate is only 54 L/minute (12 gpm). However, circulating the swimming pool water through the heat exchanger with the hot glycol and through the sand filter, required 450 W at low speed or 115 L/minute (25 gpm) and 1075 W at high speed or 350 L/minute (70 gpm). The swimming pool pump would only be operated at high speed when the extra pressure was needed to power the

Table 9.1 Monthly electrical usage and solar electricity produced kWh/month.

Load	Jan.	Feb.	Mar.	Apr.	May.	Jun.	Jul.	Aug.	Sep.	Oct.	Nov.	Dec.	kWh/Year
3rd floor fan	0	0	0	0	13	40	50	40	35	40	0	0	218
House controls	34	34	34	34	34	55	55	45	34	45	34	34	472
Pool/Cl$_2$/Sweep	72	93	112	152	194	229	198	179	175	156	92	71	1723
Refrigerator	21	21	21	21	23	27	29	24	27	24	21	21	280
Lights/computer	16	16	16	16	16	16	16	16	16	16	16	16	192
Microwave standby	7	7	7	7	7	7	7	7	7	7	7	7	84
Tel/Sec/Radio/Gar	49	49	49	49	49	49	49	49	49	49	49	49	588
Printer/FAX	12	12	12	12	12	12	12	12	12	12	12	12	144
Electric heater	11	15	0	0	0	0	0	0	0	0	11	11	48
Shop	0	0	0	0	8	25	3	0	0	0	0	0	36
Miscellaneous	0	0	0	0	0	0	0	0	0	0	0	0	0
Total and solar PV	222	247	251	291	356	460	419	372	355	349	242	221	
	71	92	111	130	134	143	143	134	130	111	92	71	
Net	151	155	140	161	222	317	276	238	225	238	150	150	2422

Time v	Jan.		Feb.		Mar.		Apr.		May.		Jun.		Jul.		Aug.		Sep.		Oct.		Nov.		Dec.	
	L	S	L	S	L	S	L	S	L	S	L	S	L	S	L	S	L	S	L	S	L	S	L	S
1:00 am	6	0	6	0	6	0	6	0	6	0	13	0	9	0	9	0	6	0	6	0	6	0	6	0
2:00 am	6	0	6	0	6	0	6	0	6	0	13	0	9	0	9	0	6	0	6	0	6	0	6	0
3:00 am	6	0	6	0	6	0	6	0	6	0	13	0	9	0	9	0	6	0	6	0	6	0	6	0
4:00 am	8	0	8	0	8	0	8	0	8	0	13	0	9	0	8	0	7	0	8	0	8	0	8	0
5:00 am	12	0	12	0	12	0	12	0	12	0	15	0	9	0	8	0	7	0	8	0	8	0	8	0
6:00 am	10	0	12	0	12	0	12	0	12	0	25	0	20	0	12	0	12	0	12	0	11	0	11	0
7:00 am	10	0	10	0	10	0	10	0	10	0	23	0	19	0	10	0	10	0	10	0	10	0	10	0
8:00 am	10	0	10	0	10	0	10	0	10	0	17	0	17	0	12	0	12	0	10	3	10	0	10	0
9:00 am	10	0	10	0	10	4	12	4	14	4	16	4	14	4	14	4	14	3	12	12	12	0	10	0
10:00 am	10	9	12	6	12	8	13	8	16	8	16	8	16	13	16	13	16	16	14	18	12	6	10	6
11:00 am	13	17	12	12	12	15	12	17	16	18	16	18	16	20	16	18	16	18	17	19	12	6	10	9
12:00 pm	14	18	16	18	16	19	20	21	22	22	22	23	22	23	22	22	22	21	21	20	16	17	13	17
1:00 pm	12	17	18	19	19	20	22	22	25	25	25	24	25	24	25	23	25	25	22	25	18	18	14	18
2:00 pm	10	10	18	18	19	19	21	21	27	27	27	27	27	25	27	25	27	25	21	25	18	18	12	17
3:00 pm	9	0	15	15	15	11	17	10	26	26	26	26	26	26	27	18	26	27	18	27	17	12	10	10
4:00 pm	9	0	7	0	11	8	10	9	26	26	26	26	26	13	26	12	26	26	13	26	8	8	7	7
5:00 pm	16	0	9	0	9	3	16	3	25	3	25	3	25	3	25	3	25	25	13	25	7	3	9	0
6:00 pm	12	0	16	0	16	0	16	1	25	0	25	0	25	0	25	0	25	0	25	0	9	0	9	0
7:00 pm	12	0	12	0	12	0	12	0	16	0	22	0	22	0	16	0	16	0	16	0	16	0	16	0
8:00 pm	10	0	10	0	10	0	10	0	14	0	20	0	20	0	14	0	14	0	14	0	12	0	12	0
9:00 pm	7	0	7	0	7	0	7	0	9	0	15	0	20	0	9	0	9	0	14	0	10	0	10	0
10:00 pm	6	0	6	0	6	0	6	0	9	0	15	0	15	0	9	0	9	0	9	0	6	0	7	0
11:00 pm	6	0	6	0	6	0	6	0	8	0	14	0	10	0	9	0	8	0	8	0	6	0	6	0
12:00 am	6	0	6	0	6	0	6	0	6	0	13	0	9	0	9	0	6	0	6	0	6	0	6	0

	Jan.	Feb.	Mar.	Apr.	May.	Jun.	Jul.	Aug.	Sep.	Oct.	Nov.	Dec.	kWh/Year
Total load	222	247	251	291	356	460	419	372	355	349	242	221	3785
Total solar PV	71	92	111	130	134	143	143	134	130	111	92	71	1362
Energy generation Present net-metering ($)	17.40	17.86	16.13	21.09	25.73	42.16	36.71	31.65	21.60	31.65	17.40	17.40	296.78
TOU net-metering ($)	14.35	14.73	13.30	15.30	16.63	24.26	21.02	17.88	16.82	17.49	14.25	14.25	200.27

Notes: Numbers in white indicates peak period, noon to 6 pm for May 2 through October 31, which includes weekdays at 32.5¢/kWh and weekends at 9.5¢/kWh.

underwater pool sweep unit. The Chlorinator, that will be discussed later, required 1075 W to manufacture the chlorine using electrochemical reactions with very low salt content of the water. So these are the three main components of the third row in the upper part of the table. Note that the load is much greater in the summer when the pool was in operation and the chlorine demand the greatest.

The next largest load came from parasitic residual loads from small appliances that are plugged into the outlets drawing small amounts of power like 3–5 W each, throughout a day. Much to the author's horror, a very large number of these small transformers plugged into the outlets included telephones, security system, radios, watering systems, tools, etc. This is a warning for the solar homeowner, to minimize these parasitic loads.

The next largest loads are the fans and automatic controls operating the various solar systems as shown in the first two rows in the upper part of Table 9.1. There is one large attic fan for nocturnal cooling that draws 228 W at high speed during summer hours with increased demand. It can also operate at lower speed during lower cooling demand. The variation over the year is shown in the table as 3rd floor fan, which is the attic fan.

Finally, at the bottom of the upper portion of this table, are shown two numbers for each month: the total load and the amount of solar PV electricity produced each month throughout the year. This power is generated when there is clear weather, light clouds or fog and varies with the number of hours of sunshine and the lower angle of the sun during winter.

In the lower portion of the table, there two numbers covering total load as "L" and PV electricity as "S" detailed for each hour of the day. Figure 9.1 shows a typical variation in PV electricity generated for each hour of the day during a peak summer day (June 22, 1999) with average atmospheric clarity. However, there can be higher output when there is only very light fog or haze that makes the sky much brighter than normal. The author has recorded many days where 16% increases over this typical summer curve have been observed with a brighter sky from light fog or haze. Of course, heavy fog or haze greatly reduces the output.

To illustrate the net electricity supplied from the grid, Figure 9.2 shows a plot of the monthly demand of electricity from the grid for the year of 2001. This is the difference between the utility meter moving forward indicating demand from the power line grid and the time the meter turns backward when solar PV power is being fed back onto the grid. The cost of this small amount of power is only about half of the total utility bill of $296.78, the remaining portion of which includes taxes,

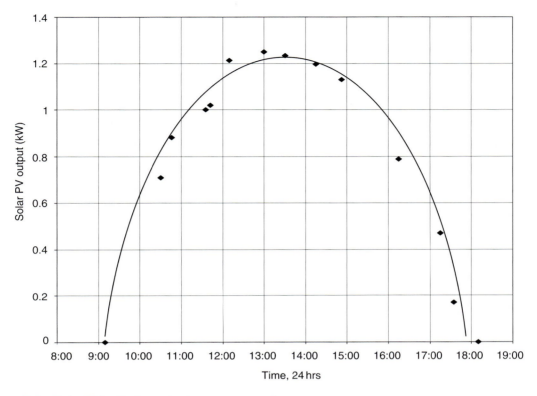

Figure 9.1 Solar PV collector output on a summer day.

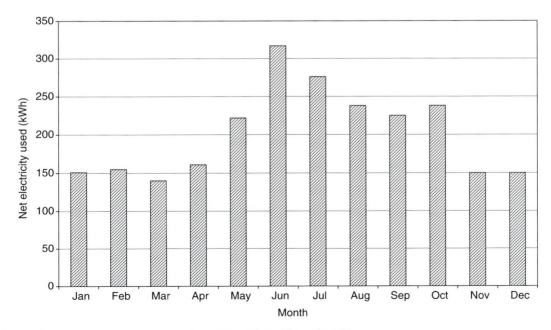

Figure 9.2 Annual net electric power usage reduced by solar PV.

fees, nuclear plant recovery, deregulation transition charges, etc. Even so, this is very low annual electricity consumption. This is particularly significant when one of the larger electric power consumers involve operating a heated swimming pool from March 1 to November 15.

The economics in favor of generating solar PV electric power fed to the grid are very significant. As of now, the credit for electricity during on-peak is 32.5¢/kWh while off-peak is only 9.5¢/kWh. In order, to initiate "grid-tied TOU net-metering", the home must be fitted with a dual meter that will track the electric power generation and consumption on two different totalizer readouts. In this way, the utility can read (manually with a meter reader visit or by telephone line interface) both scales. In the monthly billing, the on-peak credit at 32.5¢/kWh is applied against the usage cost at 9.5¢/kWh during off-peak. At the end of the year, there is a "true-up" calculation that examines the whole year performance. If there is a net consumption of electricity (off-peak minus on-peak), then the small residual is billed at a lower rate of 9.5¢/kWh. If there is a net generation fed into the grid (on-peak minus off-peak a positive number), then in California, this power must be "donated" to the utility. That is, the solar PV generating homeowner gets no financial payment for this electric power. Thus, it is clear that the optimum is to just produce a near balance, with off-peak equal to on-peak.

The bottom line in Table 9.1 shows the comparison if the system were on the utility's TOU net-metering billing rate structure. For solar systems with this rate structure, there are substantial savings, since for this case the annual electricity charge would be only $200.27. As attractive as "grid-tied TOU net-metering" clearly is, one must be very cautious in signing up for this change, as there is a $298 charge initially for the new, two-way, dual scale meter. So it is a good idea to compute the improvement to make sure the added cost of this special meter is justified. For the case of the Berkeley house, yearly savings of $91.51 will payback the cost of this meter in about 4 years – a very good investment indeed.

9.2   STAND-ALONE SYSTEMS AND ENERGY STORAGE OPTIONS

The Berkeley solar house PV system was sized so, that about 1.8 kW of capacity rated collectors were installed as a grid-connected system. From the analysis above, it can be seen that they actually achieve about 36% or 1368 kWh/year of the annual total electric load covered by solar PV. This fraction was limited by the available roof area.

If this system was not connected to the grid, an energy storage option would be required and the solar PV collectors would have to be nearly tripled in the numbers of collectors to provide 100% of the power demand. For those States without rebates, this would be a significant cost at $5.50 per peak watt of PV collector capacity installed. For the case of the Berkeley house, this would add to the cost of the collectors with the State $4 per peak watt rebate – a total of $5400. Then in addition, there is the capital cost of providing enough electric power storage batteries to handle the maximum average load of 460 kWh per month as shown in Table 9.1 that occurs in June, which is 618 W on an average.

So for sizing the batteries, the experience from DHW discussed earlier suggests that 4 days of storage would be near optimum, or 2472 W, or 4944 W, for batteries that will have a long life at 50% depth of discharge. If the batteries are located where the weather can reach low temperatures, the batteries must be derated (Jade, 2002) significantly as shown in Table 9.2.

In California in the summer time, there would be no derating needed, but in colder areas where the batteries would be stored at a cold temperature at the time of a large demand, then the derating would be significant.

The last step in sizing of battery requirement is to take the battery capacity needed, like the 4944 W example given, and select batteries with different amp-hour rating (such as, from Jade, 2002). For example, if one selected a DEKA, deep cycle battery of 12 V at 265 amp-hours, the number of batteries needed would be 4944 W/(12 V × 265 amp-hour) = 1.6 batteries or 2 batteries. This would cost about $800 or $162/kW. If one selects a large 2 V IBE Industrial battery at 1530 amp-hours, then 2 batteries would be needed, costing around US $870.

The batteries discussed above have a 5-year warranty and would need to be replaced as part of the operating cost. Over their life, the capital cost replacement every 5-years added

Table 9.2 Battery derating.

Temperature		Derating factor
°C	°F	
26.6	80	1.00
21.1	70	1.04
15.6	60	1.11
10.0	50	1.19
4.4	40	1.30
−1.1	30	1.40
−6.7	20	1.50

about 0.02¢/kWh to the solar PV electric generation cost. There would also be added costs of maintaining the batteries, which is estimated to triple this cost to about 0.06¢/kWh.

A futuristic battery is the Nickel Metal Hydride battery from GM/Ovonics producing 13.6 V at 85 amp-hours. For this battery, 4.27 or 5 batteries would be needed at a cost of $11,000 for the new ones or $3000 for the re-qualified. The reason this battery is preferred over the lead-acid or alkali type is that it performs at low temperature, and there is no maintenance problem and no environmental impact with the materials of construction over its life cycle. It also has a long warranty of about 15 years. Replacing the re-qualified battery every 15 years would add about 0.02¢/kWh to the solar PV electric generation cost since there would be insignificant maintenance. So even though this battery is much more expensive, it is considerably more cost-effective over its life. In fact, even the entirely new battery would be more cost-effective than the other two above. This may not appear obvious when considering the large initial capital outlay.

Besides batteries, there are other energy storage technologies that would enable the solar PV system to avoid connecting to the grid of which flywheel is the first. A flywheel UPS system is manufactured by Caterpillar and comes in sizes from 150 to 900 kVA sizes that supply from 5 to 30 kWh. The largest of these would only supply 3 days of summer or 6 days of winter loads shown in Table 9.1 without a diesel engine-generator set. These units are really designed for providing 15-second "ride-through" times for a standard diesel engine-generator set to crank, start-up, and pick up the full load up to 900 kVA. The costs for this complete system are around $40/kVA. Since these costs are one-quarter that of conventional batteries that are $162/kW, one should consider the advantages of elimination of batteries over the diesel genset based system, that functions without any gap in power when the solar source is not available. One must remember that the diesel engine consumes diesel fuel at $14.4/GJ ($14.4/million Btu) and contributes about 5.18¢/kWh to a total amortized generation cost of about 20¢/kWh when engine maintenance, oil, and operational testing is considered.

It is also possible to use a natural gas-fueled engine. However, a warning about the rapidly fluctuating costs of natural gas is in order. At present (Johnson, 2003), natural gas at wholesale prices costs $6/GJ ($6/million Btu), which itself contributes 2.16¢/kWh without any delivery. Also a natural gas-fueled diesel engine operates at about half the efficiency of a diesel engine. So when all the savings and added expenses are taken into account, the generation costs between the two engine-driven generator sets are about comparable.

Both are however noisy, while diesel besides noise expels bad-smelling exhaust. Natural gas can be supplied by pipeline and boosted with a small compressor, whereas the diesel must be stored in an ugly above-ground tank that is fire-protected.

The most exciting new alternative to batteries and engine-driven generators are fuel cells which can be powered by natural gas or on-site stored propane. The fuel cells can be purchased in a range of sizes appropriate for homes from the Fuel Cell Store[1]. Plug-Power of New York has been recently manufacturing and marketing such systems with General Electric, as installer and service organizations are becoming of increased interest. The costs are around US $30,000/kW and therefore more expensive than the Caterpillar* flywheel UPS. But there is great hope that these fuel cell costs would rapidly drop off. For example, in large production manufacturing scales their costs are expected to drop to $1250/kW. The electric power generation costs would be around 20¢/kWh.

The flywheel or the ultra-capacitor systems have limited capacity to store solar PV energy and a straight engine-driven generator has no storage capability at all with excess solar. But in the case of fuel cells, the recently emerging "reversible fuel cells" can use hydrogen and produce power or can be fed direct current electricity from solar PV collectors and make hydrogen from water. In other words, they can work backward like an electrolysis unit. The hydrogen can be stored on-site and therefore store huge quantities of solar energy to be used when it is needed at night or in cloudy weather. More discussions about these fuel cells will be discussed in Chapter 14.

The futuristic case of the fuel cell car that shares its fuel cell when it is parked at and plugged into the house will be discussed in Chapter 14. Such a fuel cell manufactured in a huge scale for vehicles, would be expected to drop its cost down to $50/kW.

9.3   SIZING PV FOR HOUSE LOADS

Selecting the proper size of the solar PV collector system is not easy and requires a good understanding of the time dependence of the home loads and how they match with solar PV output. Such a study was done on the Berkeley house and is shown in the lower portion of Table 9.1 and the solar home planner must include this type of proforma analysis.

For a grid-connected solar PV system, the matching of the loads to the solar PV output is important to minimize the net

---

*Caterpillar, Peoria, IL (2002) with dealers over the whole world.

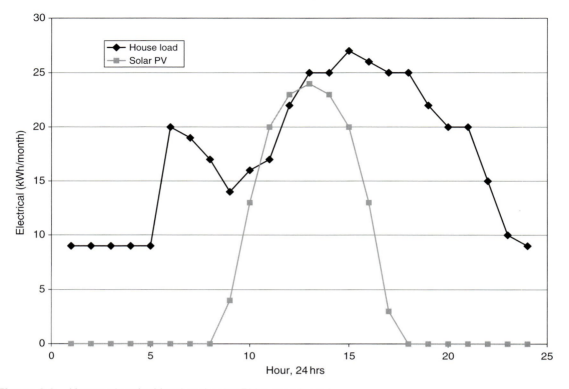

Figure 9.3   House electrical load and solar PV output for July.

electric power used during the most expensive on-peak period of noon to 6 pm during summer. This matching of the load and solar PV has been shown in Figure 9.3 for July. Note that there is an early morning load from kitchen and lighting. There is a late night load from fans operating to cool the house, or if the night air is too hot for house cooling, then the heat pump air conditioner must be used which raised the load even more. The solar PV electricity generation begins a little after 9 am and begins significant power generation at 10 am. It continues until about 6 pm (18:00 hrs) and then drops off quickly as the sun sets. Also in July there are a significant number of days with morning fog that effectively delays the month's solar electric power in the morning, so that the average peak is shifted away from 1 pm towards 2 pm. The collector, tilted at 45°, faces southwest so that more solar energy is extracted from the afternoon sun, when there is less chance for fog. This effect shows by the shifting of the solar PV output.

A load/solar PV comparison for December when the solar energy received is the least is also shown. Figure 9.4 shows the time trends of both. It can be noted that in the winter time there is added lighting and heating load in the early morning

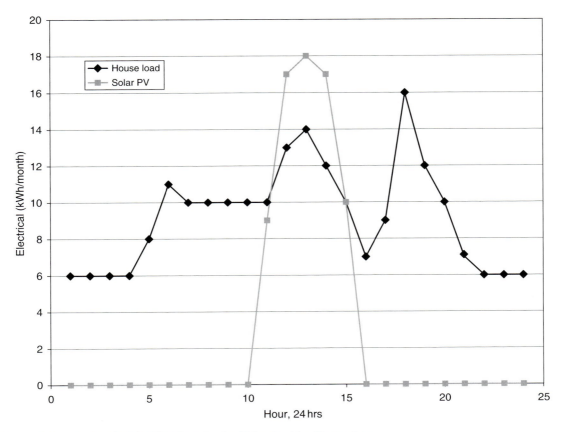

Figure 9.4   House electrical load and solar PV output for December.

and evening when there is no solar and no large cooling energy demand as in the summer months.

9.4   LOAD SHIFTING OPTIONS

Another reason for orienting the solar PV collectors more towards southwest is to get more of the solar PV energy into the on-peak noon to 6 pm period to offset the higher TOU net-metering billing rates. This is one critical action that can be taken to do some load shifting so that solar PV can offset electric load during this on-peak period.

An example of load shifting is the rescheduling of electric demands occurring in the more expensive on-peak period to move them to the cheaper off-peak period. Electric appliances such as washing, electric microwave cooking, vacuuming, pool filtering, fans, air conditioning, etc. can be used during the off-peak period whenever possible. Referring to Figure 9.3 for the month of July, it would be most helpful to shift the fan cooling and/or air conditioning load in the afternoon and early evening (between 1 and 6 pm) to occur after 6 pm when the rates are cheaper. Again referring to Figure 9.3, if there were more solar collectors and more solar PV, it would be sensible to shift this afternoon cooling mode to occur earlier from say 10 am to 6 pm so that it is coincident with the solar PV output if it were larger and would avoid any on-peak loads.

In fact, the time period of 9 am to noon is excellent for cooling load shifting, since under TOU net-metering electric power is only at 9.5¢/kWh. If the outside air is cooler than the house, cool air can be pulled into the house and used to cool down as much thermal mass as possible. At noon, the fans are turned off and the house is sealed. In this way, the cool thermal mass keeps the house cooler throughout the on-peak period of noon to 6 pm. If the outside air rises above the house temperature, then the heat pump air conditioning system is operated to cool down the house thermal mass up to the noontime cutoff. It is clear that it is more cost-effective to run fans or air conditioning when the power is cheap rather than later, when it is more expensive. This is another motivation for incorporating substantial thermal mass in the design of the house.

A very sophisticated load shifting cooling concept, although expensive, is off-peak ice-making. These machines operate a freezer at night that produces ice outside heat exchanger tubes. When there is a need for air conditioning, the cooled water is run through these tubes to produce cooling for the HVAC system to cool the house. This ice-making approach is usually done only in large commercial buildings that are occupied during the day and unoccupied at night. However, it is a great example of load shifting.

In future, when reversible fuel cells are commercially available, the cheaper off-peak power can be used to operate the fuel cell in reverse to produce hydrogen which is stored in a hydride bed. Then when there is an electrical demand, such as for cooling, during the on-peak period, the hydrogen can be pulled out of the storage to drive the fuel cell forward to make electricity.

The above three examples are just a sampling of creative ideas that can be put to play for accomplishing load-shifting for reducing energy costs and helping the public utilities handle their peak load problems.

9.5   PV COLLECTORS WITH INTEGRAL HOT WATER HEATING (PV/T)

The industry standard rating of solar PV collectors involves providing the efficiency at 25°C (77°F) of converting solar

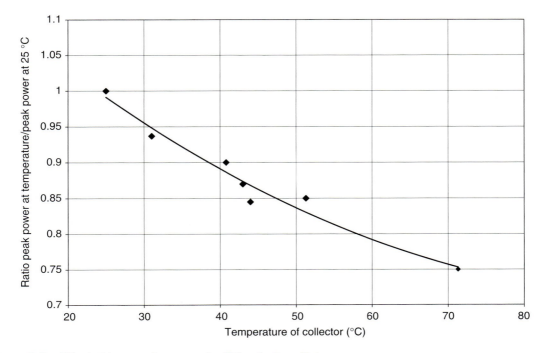

Figure 9.5   Effect of temperature on solar PV collector efficiency.

insolation to electrical power output using a standard insolation rate of 1000 W/m². These efficiencies should be printed on the certification label affixed to the collector. For the ASE America's Model DG300 PV collectors this efficiency is 13%. Their collectors are one of the highest efficiency in the industry today. However, this efficiency drops with increasing temperature about 0.5% per centigrade (ASE Americas, 1998). This major effect is shown in Figure 9.5.

In the early testing immediately after installation of the solar PV collectors with insolation rate of 1 kW/m² on many summer days, produced a collector temperature of 57°C (135°F) with the back side of the collector completely open to the wind for cooling at ambient temperatures around 24°C (75°F). This is significantly warmer than the 25°C at which the efficiency was established and power output affixed on a nameplate. At 1 kW/m² insolation, the panel temperature is 33°C (91.4°F) above ambient. Also, the efficiency typically falls from 13% down to 10.7%. It would be most helpful to have the collector cooled.

Active cooling of the solar PV collectors should be able to restore the collector thermal state to the desired and rated 25°C for which the higher efficiency is achieved. And further, this recovered heat can be used for a variety of purposes such as space heating in a building for heating DHW or swimming pools.

Lower collector temperatures extend the life of the glass, PV sandwich, and backing, since the sealants and insulation will last longer. This will make possible an extended warranty period of performance beyond the presently specified 10 years.

The author used a small ASE-50 (ASE-050-DG/17#6040) collector for testing this cooling and heat recovery concept. Such a combined collector that produces both electric power as well as thermal energy is called a "PV/T collector." On the back of this collector a copper tube coil heat exchanger was thermally bonded so that cool water circulating through these coil tubes quickly cooled the collector close to the water temperature. This transferred water temperature circulated was varied to produce a range of collector temperatures from 31°C to 71.3°C (88–160°F). The efficiency effect was shown in Figure 9.5. The difference in water temperature in and out was only 6°C to 7°C (11°F to 13.4°F) at water flow rates from 410 to 490 ml/min. The solar insolation was measured at the collector for each of the tests and it averaged around 950 W/m². To ensure the accuracy of the measurements of temperature and flowrates, a heat balance was made and it closed from 90.8% to 106.5%. So there is an account for where all the heat went.

These commercial ASE Americas collectors consist of the silicon cells sandwiched between two sealed sheets of clear glass. Since the glass plates of the PV collector are not very conductive, an estimate had to be made of the worst-case temperature gradient perpendicular through the glass to remove the heat flux generated by the front surface insolation. The glass was assumed to be 4.76 mm plate glass with a thermal conductivity, $k = 0.76$ W/m-°K, the 0.5 mm plastic adhesive with a $k = 0.232$ W/m-°K, and 0.25 mm of silicon with a $k = 8$ W/m-°K. Assuming the test specification insolation of 1 kW/m² with 13% of this being converted to electrical energy that is removed from the panel, the thermal flux of 0.878 kW/m² was taken through the depth of the panel to the back. The gradient was calculated as 14.7°C (58.5°F) using two glass plates, two plastic adhesive layers, and the silicon crystal as detailed above. To maintain the silicon crystal layer at 25°C (77°F), the back glass surface temperature had to be 17.7°C (64°F).

Given the above heat transfer situation, the feasibility of using a glycol–water mixture as the heat transfer fluid should be examined first. For the full-size collector of 2.4 m², the glycol–water flow needed to remove the heat is about 0.125 kg/s (2 gpm), assuming that a ΔT of 5°C (9°F) rise in the glycol–water mixture is tolerated. If the heat exchanger tube internal diameter is 7.5 mm, then the internal velocity will be 3.4 m/s or a Reynolds number (Re) of 25,500. So we conclude that this cooling is feasible. So the best use of this fluid at 17.7°C (64°F) need to be considered.

Thus, there are significant internal PV collector thermal resistances that must be carefully addressed in order to prevent undesirable heat build-up. If borosilicate glass is used, its thermal conductivity is $k = 1.09\,W/m^2\text{-}^\circ K$, which is 43% better than plate glass. Also a large improvement of 7°C (13°F) could be achieved if the bottom glass sheet were replaced with conductive aluminum.

Armed with these conclusions, the testing was repeated on February 1, 1999 with a different ASE Americas collector specially manufactured with a conductive aluminum foil backing. The performance was definitely improved, as predicted by the analysis above. In fact, the collector could be dropped in temperature down to 29.5°C (85.1°F) with water circulating on its backside at 15.28°C (59.5°F). In conclusion, the aluminum foil backing on the solar collector allowed its temperature to be dropped below the test on the double glass plate collector and achieve a 15.5% improvement in PV performance.

So now consider how creatively one can use this large quantity of heat energy at 17.7°C (64°F) from the PV/T collector to do something useful in the solar house. First, consider a standard commercial water-source heat pump (with SUVA®, ozone-friendly Freon HCFC-123® that replaced Freon-11®) that will accept the liquid glycol at 17.7°C (64°F), boil it, and boost its temperature to 71.3°C (160°F). This will provide both DHW as well as hot water for space heating. If the tank could be highly stratified, a single tank would provide all the DHW the house could use off the top of the tank and hot water for heating the radiant floors off the middle of the tank. After this heat is extracted, the output of the heat pump would return cold glycol at 12.7°C (55°F) back to the solar PV collector for cooling.

So now getting even colder. So further, with the coolant water circulating at 5°C (41°F), the collector could be cooled down to 19°C (66°F), at which temperature the collector efficiency would be increased higher than on the nameplate, up to 13.4%.

So finally an even more futuristic concept to use this large quantity of heat energy at this lower temperature of 5°C (41°F) from the PV/T collector to do something useful in the solar house should be considered. Initially, a standard commercial water-source heat pump (using Freon® with a lower boiling point) that will accept the 5°C (41°F) glycol, boil it, and boost its temperature to 61°C (142°F) to provide both DHW as well as hot water for space heating is taken. With mechanical improvements in heat pumps, it might be possible in the future to achieve a slightly higher temperature of DHW. The same highly stratified, single tank could still be used.

Economic analysis of a 7.5 kW solar PV house

The purpose of this section is to describe the results of the most challenging application involving a single-family residence in moderate climate using 25 ASE Americas 300 W$_{peak}$ collectors with heat recovery backplates. For this application, there were about 180 heat-degree days and 180 cooling-degree days. The heating and cooling are supplied by a commercially available heat pump (ClimateMaster Model WE036 water-to-water 3-ton unit) for $1960 in 1998 for single units and $1860 for units of >10. However, this heat pump is not installed for conventional use, instead it is installed to utilize the waste heat from the solar PV/T collectors via a heat recovery backplate presented in the previous sections.

This house has installed 25 solar PV collectors on the roof optimized for winter heating. Each PV collector is fitted with this heat recovery backplate that extracts the waste heat and maintains the solar module PV cells at 20°C (68°F) or below. As shown in the previous sections, these solar PV collectors would normally operate at 50°C (122°F) with a solar insolation-to-electrical efficiency of only 8.35%. However, when operated at 20°C (68°F) with this heat recovery backplate, they produce electricity at 13.39% – nearly double!!

To illustrate how this makes a solar PV house feasible in today's economy, an hourly simulation was done using a typical DHW load, space heating load, and electrical load. Each of these loads is provided by the solar insolation, which generates PV electricity output and thermal output from the heat recovery backplate. In cases where the house requires heating, the heated glycol at <20°C (<68°F) from the backplate is fed to the source-side of the heat pump. The thermodynamic organic cycle in the commercial heat pump cited above raises this temperature to 48.9°C (120°F) for DHW and space heating. The heat pump electrical load is supplied by the PV/T collectors, since it is operated entirely in phase with the solar insolation. To cover cloudy days and night time, hot water is stored in a highly insulated 7.5 m³ (2000 gallon) tank that measures only 2 m in diameter by 2.43 m tall (6.5 ft diameter by 8 ft tall). This thermal storage tank provides about a week of energy capacity.

In cases where the house requires cooling, the heat pump cycle is reversed and operated at nighttime. In this mode, the PV/T collector backplates serve as a heat rejection function into the cooler night air. The heat pump cools the glycol in the cooling loop to the coolth storage tank at 10–15.6°C (50–60°F). This tank is identical in size to the heat storage tank above. During a hot day that requires house cooling, the HVAC system in the house will be fed with cool glycol from this tank.

For the climate requiring 180 cooling-degree days, this tank will have about a week of capacity.

Regarding the typical decline in PV collector performance over time, the coupling of the heat pump should greatly alleviate this problem. The improvement in electricial efficiency by operating the PV/T collector at <20°C (<68°F) should provide operating experience that this excellent performance would continue for 20 years and maybe 30 years without the typical 10% degradation in 10 years. This means that this solar-heat pump installation will show a net dollar savings every year over a conventional all-electric heat pump house. To prove this, an economic analysis follows.

The technology investment includes 25 ASE Americas 300 W_{peak} collectors fitted with the heat recovery backplate at \$4.50/W_{peak} or \$33,750 with selective-coating on the cover glass for an added \$1000, the ClimateMaster W036 heat pump at \$2000, the PV/T collector roof mounting at \$7500, the 8 kW inverter at \$5000, two glycol–water pumps at \$500, two 7.5 m^3 storage tanks at \$4000, and automatic controls at \$1500 – totaling \$55,215. This capital investment is financed by special World Bank solar PV financing at 4% interest over 30 years for \$3253.12 per year payments or over 20 years for \$4206.66 per year. With a \$3/W_{peak} rebate, now in most US states (some as high as \$4.50), the financed capital cost becomes \$31,750. Accordingly, these yearly financing payments would become \$1928.32 and \$2493.55, respectively for 30 and 20 years.

For comparison, the base case conventional all-electric house with the same heat pump alone and no solar PV would have a yearly cost of \$3333.00, assuming that the heat pump is included in the house mortgage. The annual savings of the solar PV/T heat pump house over the conventional house are \$1404.68 for the 30-year loan and \$839.45 for the 20-year loan. Comparing the two, this shows a payback of the installation in 22 years for the 30-year loan case, which would be justified.

Finally, just a quick mention of the same analysis done for a 225 solar PV/T collector 10-unit condominium and all the economics look even better. The heat pump is larger (ClimateMaster WE120 water-to-water 10-ton unit) available for only \$3960 for single units and \$3860 for units of >10. Also there is economy of scale on all other components.

There are occasional studies of PV/T system in buildings around the world.

There are two published technical papers of note. The first covers integrating PV/T collectors into a building to provide electricity and space heating with and without heat pumps (Bazillian, 2001). The second covers an experimental performance study of mounting a PV collector onto a plastic swimming pool collector to remove heat (Sandnes, 2002). Both papers corroborate the presentation in the sections of this chapter above but do not study the heat pump advantages in the economics for a house or a condo.

The whole field of PV/T collectors and their development will be an exciting area to watch as new advances become possible.

9.6   PRESENT RESEARCH LEADING TO CHEAPER/ HIGH EFFICIENCY FUTURE PV COLLECTORS

The Sanyo Electric Co., Osaka, Japan has developed a new PV system based on Hetero-junction with Intrinsic Thin-layer technology (HIT) that provides very high efficiencies just over 15%, has no problem decline with increasing temperature (Sanyo, 2002). They are marketing now in Europe.

Powerlight Corporation, Berkeley, CA is the largest solar PV provider for commercial buildings in the US and is one of the most rapidly growing solar companies as well. It has installed 7 MW of solar PV last year and is well on its way to install 10 MW this year. It has just installed their first insulated roof panel system incorporating the new Sanyo HIT PV collectors (discussed above) with high efficiency (Powerlight, 2003). Their insulating foam roof tiles are interlocking and have a system of electrical interfacing that is neat and compact and ideally suited for a flat roof and mounts without any roof penetrations.

AstroPower[2] has unveiled a new product line that provides an integrated roof top that includes solar PV (AstroPower, 2002). These fully integrate into a residential roof-top. The benefits involve faster installation time, lower cost, and enhanced appearance. The product aligns with existing roof shingles to create a seamless roof appearance. It is aimed at homebuilders including: Shea Homes, Pardee Homes, Premier Homes, Centrex, Standard Pacific of San Diego, Clarum Homes, and US Home.

UniSolar[3] also provides a solar shingle roof solar PV product that is based on a thin film that is a foil, assembled into a shingle that can be laid with a conventional shingle roof. It blends very well with the roof-top and is only slightly noticeable from its higher gloss. The market and sales are beginning to grow, as the product becomes known with homebuilders.

On March 25, 2003 BP Solar announced its new line of PV collectors made with a mosaic of 125 mm size cells each with an efficiency of 18.3% (verified by the Fraunhofer Institute Solar Energiesysteme, Germany). This is the current world record in efficiency. There are continual improvements in solar PV efficiency and lowering of costs to move the world to a very bright solar PV future.

ENDNOTES

1. Fuel Cell Store in Boulder, Colorado (www.fuelcellstore.com).
2. AstroPower, www.astropower.com
3. UniSolar manufactures the thin film PV collectors with multiple layers to absorb a broader range of warelenth than crytalline PV collectors (www.unisolar.com, www.ovonic.com/unisolar.htm)

Annual energy use

10

10.1 Berkeley house
10.2 Comparison of EU and US

10.1 BERKELEY HOUSE

Calculating the annual energy use for Berkeley house is easy since there is no significant natural gas used. The energy use has been detailed for each month of the year by major electrical demand and also the solar PV electricity produced (see Table 9.1). Solar PV-generated electricity supplies power for the entire swimming pool equipment, including the large 240 V AC, 1.5 hp pool water-circulating pump, filtering the pool water as well as chlorinating the water and heating it via the solar-heated heat exchanger, and driving the pool sweep part time. This is normally a large energy demand for a pool owner, which is completely handled with solar energy. In addition to this energy-intensive swimming pool operation, the solar PV also supplies power for the rest of the house. Electric power with any excess, reverses and spins the utility meter backward to provide a credit.

The reduced usage of electricity has been documented as per Figure 9.2 for an entire year. The total electricity-generating cost billed for entire 2002 at year-end by the utility was only US $268.00. As shown in Figure 9.2, there is a seasonal variation with more electric use during summer owing to the pool operation and cooling fans. The typical monthly electric bill was US $5.35 to cover transmission and distribution charges by the utility plus a large range of taxes of all kinds – independent of electricity generation cost.

On a floor area basis, the Berkeley house with swimming pool operation uses a total annual energy of only 8.6 kWh/m^2

per year (0.8 kWh/ft^2 per year). Since there was completely negligible use of natural gas, this figure represents the total energy use.

For the occupants of a solar house with solar thermal and solar PV, there is always satisfaction about saving energy. The automation of the solar functions, however, removes the drudgery involved in manually operating all the solar functions and making choices, sometimes on an hourly basis. As shown in earlier chapters, the color touch screen display shows the status and operations of the solar functions. Normally no changes in set-points are needed, but when there are any changes needed for visitors or vacations, this is done with a simple touch of the finger. Some future technologies will make the solar house even more enjoyable and these have been discussed in Chapter 14.

10.2   COMPARISON OF EU AND US

In the US during 1973–1984, the sudden increase in energy costs triggered a greater attention to energy management in buildings, from residential to commercial. As a result of this consciousness, buildings greatly improved in energy efficiency in aspects such as wall insulation, improved window design, improved heating and cooling systems. There were typically 40% improvements in the energy efficiency of commercial buildings [Solar Energy Research Institute, 1988, pg. 9] to an annual 126 kWh/m^2 (40 kBtu/ft^2) and a similar improvement in new or rebuilt residential buildings to an annual 25 kWh/m^2 (8 kBtu/ft^2).

In addition to these dramatic energy efficiency improvements in building construction technology, there have recently been improvements in energy management, with set back thermostats, improved appliance efficiency, occupancy sensors, and improving occupant attention to saving energy as a fundamental philosophy. As has been recently demonstrated in California during severe energy shortages of electric power, residential owners were able to save consistently 25% as just being more diligent in energy usage in their daily activities. Although no hard data was found, it is believed that energy reductions for residential buildings have recently dropped to an annual 15 kWh/m^2 (4.8 kBtu/ft^2). This compares most favorably to the energy-efficient European house of 15–30 kWh/m^2 per year (EUREC, 2002).

On a floor area basis, the Berkeley house with swimming pool operation uses a total annual energy of only 8.6 kWh/m^2 per year (0.8 kWh/ft^2 per year). Since there was absolutely negligible use of natural gas, this figure represents the total

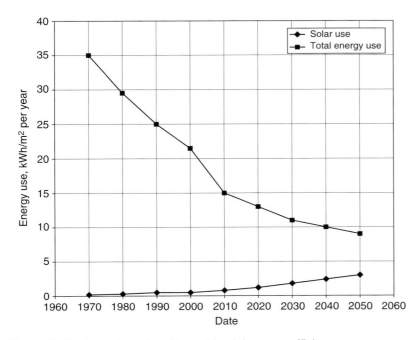

Figure 10.1   Long-term trend in residential energy efficiency.

energy use. Above all, further reductions in residential energy use can be made when solar energy or wind are used as local energy generation sources. As seen in Chapter 6, the Berkeley house had about 25% of its annual electrical energy use supplied by solar PV.

In the US 25–40% improvements in residential efficiency have been noticed immediately following 2000 as can be seen in Figure 10.1. In addition, a continuing trend is foreseen where the US residential housing stock will continue to move toward high energy efficiency and will join the already high efficiency EU housing. This trend is projected in Figure 10.1 for total energy use over many decades toward 2050 when the residential energy efficiency is expected to reach about 9 kWh/m^2 per year, with around 25–30% of residential energy coming from solar passive design elements as well as active solar thermal and PV. So a bright solar future is ahead worldwide.

11

Maintenance saves money

11.1 Preventative maintenance schedule
11.2 Stable major suppliers
11.3 Experience record

11.1 PREVENTATIVE MAINTENANCE SCHEDULE

Preventative maintenance (PM), is a very important aspect of the solar house in keeping the operation at peak efficiency and in preserving one's capital investment. On the whole, solar collectors, whether they are thermal collectors or PV, maintenance is nearly negligible. Only twice a year after a dry and dusty summer, in early evening when the sun is down, a strong jet of water from the garden house will wash off any dust on their surfaces. The solar PV inverter is completely maintenance free. In fact the inverter operates without any attention for long that the homeowner often neglects even looking at its little control panel display. If there is an error of any type, a red light is displayed, which is the only attention given to the inverter.

The PM routine is best done with outside contractors (preferably one company) who are familiar with all the operational characteristics of the equipment and their idiosyncrasies and who has stocked parts on their truck and knows the faster way for their replacement. The author had personally done maintenance on the equipment and learnt that it was more cost-effective for the PM to be done by the suppliers and highly recommended that it should be carefully considered.

Regularly checking the equipment operation in each of the particular modes, be it radiant floor heating, greenhouse heating, nocturnal cooling, heat pump cooling, etc., is an important part of PM. The checking should involve listing items that are in need of urgent service or those that can be covered in the next regular PM cycle. Leaks from joints and fittings are normally small and can be noted to be fixed in a regular PM cycle. Pump failure can be indicated by its flow-meter, showing low or no flow, by the motor overheating. Automatic valves sometimes get jammed from debris dislodged in the glycol systems and fail to position correctly and the flow-meters show this failure quickly. Air-handling systems are best checked by visually checking the vent dampers with regard to position, airflow into the various thermal zone spaces, and the temperature of the spaces compared to their control set-point. Another very valuable diagnostic check can be made by examining the plotting or trending of temperatures and looking for sudden changes in temperature or relationships that make no sense.

The rest of the solar system that involves the thermal components requires routine PM to insure their proper operation. The equipment supplier selected is an important part of achieving a good operational and maintenance experience, since they remain in business, supply parts when needed, and are available to provide important technical advice on the piece of equipment involved. This aspect is discussed in Section 11.2. Since the Berkeley house has operated continuously for a decade, it is possible to detail the maintenance record listed in Section 11.3.

11.2   STABLE MAJOR SUPPLIERS

Selecting stable major equipment suppliers is a very important decision that one should make for their solar house. The longevity of equipment suppliers is much more likely when the company is large, has a broad range of products, and is one of the largest volume suppliers of the item. Solar equipment design and installation companies have a solid experience with solar equipment and can very confidently make invaluable recommendations regarding supplier and equipment model. The equipment selected is an important part of achieving a good operational and maintenance experience. A major equipment manufacturer is more likely to supply parts when needed, and available to provide important technical advice on the piece of equipment involved.

Such outstanding suppliers are as follows:

1. Wirsbo – makers of radiant floor valves
2. TACO – thermal actuated valves
3. Honeywell – motor valves
4. Compool – actuating ball valves, sand filter and two-speed pump
5. Red-White Valve Corp. – hand operated ball valves

6. TACO – cartridge magnetic drive pumps
7. TACO – check valves and regulator valves
8. Red-White – rotometers for fluid flow
9. Letro – dial thermometers
10. Goldline – thermistors
11. Spirovent – removes entrained air bubbles
12. Heliodyne – solar thermal collectors
14. ASE Americas – solar PV collectors (now RWE Schott Solar, Inc.)
15. Trace Engineering – for solar PV inverter
16. Vent Axia – fans
17. Invensys – automatic control hardware and software systems

11.3   EXPERIENCE RECORD

A decade of operating the Berkeley solar house has made it possible to detail the maintenance record. At the 3-year point the most frequently operated Vent Axia duct fan failed only after 4000 hours of operation. The manufacturer recognized this electric motor bearing defect in their production and replaced the electric motor with an oil-less bearing of long life. The replacement unit has operated flawlessly ever since. A Honeywell motor-actuated valve failed at the highest temperature application in the hot water heater after 5 years of high temperature service. The temperature set-point was reduced and the valve replaced with a TACO thermal-actuated valve. At the 10-year point, a TACO regulator valve failed and caused the total system pressure to ratchet up to unacceptably high pressures upon temperature cycling from night to day. This challenging and subtle problem was correctly identified by Sun Light and Power Co. and it was replaced. The system pressure has remained at the low set-point of 2 atm absolute pressure ever since.

In replacing several of these items, it was discovered that critical isolation valves were not installed to allow for the unit replacement, without draining the system at significant expense, glycol replacement and time. Isolation valves were installed to enable easier maintenance in the future. One of the fans in the ceiling vent ducting was installed before the sheet rock, which covered up the framework and prevented its removal. A considerable days effort was expended by the Sun Light and Power operations manager in sawing out the sheetrock and reframing around the fan and replacing the fan. This was done at no-cost in recognition of their design and installation error.

This experience has been most helpful in revealing the importance of having major equipment suppliers that stand behind their equipment, and an excellent 30-year solar company (Sun Light and Power Co.) that stands behind their design, installation and service.

Consequently, it was strongly recommended that each solar home designer, contractor, and owner insist that the design be reviewed from a maintenance standpoint to insure that critical equipment items can be replaced easily. Next, the owner should contract with a major solar company to routinely provide PM to insure long-term failure-free operation. This will save time and grief as well as money in the longer term for the life of the solar house.

12

Payback economics

12.1   STATE AND FEDERAL INCENTIVES

Local and federal governments differ over the world in their subsidies for solar energy. Generally, they are encouraged with some capital cost-reduction program to lower the initial barrier of the high cost of solar thermal and/or solar PV. In this regard, California is rather typical, with a solar hardware purchase-rebate system. The majority of the US states have such a program, as well as the Scandinavian countries, Japan, and most of EU. Many other countries are quickly following suit with such programs around the world.

In California, statewide, there is a base $3.50/peak watt rebate, whereas in Los Angeles county it is a $4.50/peak watt rebate program. These rebates are only for the capital cost of the solar PV collectors for electricity and for solar thermal collectors for space heating and DHW. Swimming pool solar heat does not qualify. The program requires that the builder make a reservation with the State's California Energy Commission under the "Solar Buy-down Program". Most solar contractors and solar equipment suppliers will happily provide the forms, filled out, for one's signature as well as theirs to reserve the funds. The buy-down program pays the solar equipment supplier once the purchase is made and is otherwise transparent to the solar homeowner. It is a very successful program. It covers solar PV thermal and fuel cells up to energy capacity levels of 1 MW at present.

Generally, it is not well advertised and so many homeowners do not know about the "Solar Buy-down Program" until they make a decision to add solar to their homes or build a solar home and contact a solar builder or solar equipment supplier. The solar buy-down reservation can be done early to hold the funds while the solar design and construction proceeds. This is a very good idea, since the homeowner would be harmed if the decision about a solar home is delayed and during the interim the solar rebate program disappears. For other States, the EU and other countries, the potential solar homeowner/builder should inquire early about such solar incentive programs.

In the design of the Berkeley solar house, we combined the solar space heating and DHW with swimming pool heating. In this way, the solar collectors that supplied solar space heating and DHW could also be used to heat the swimming pool when the first two loads were satisfied. This design approach gets around the restriction that there can be no solar rebate for solar swimming pool heat. Also the pool filter and chlorination system does not qualify, but this is a small portion of the cost.

There are no US Federal solar rebate programs proposed or likely in the near future, but tax incentives are in place and there are more coming.

12.2   TAX BENEFITS

In addition to this solar equipment rebate program, most governments have some type of tax benefit allowance for deductions or tax-credits. In many cases, these deductions can include the labor cost of installation, while others are for equipment purchases only.

In the late 1970s and early 1980s there was a State 55% tax credit for swimming pool solar thermal systems to reduce swimming pool heating by natural gas and this program was very successful. But it was not continued later on.

There are State $2500 alternative energy-tax credits for solar energy, and soon to be a Federal Tax credit program of $5000 or 20%, whichever is less (Hamer, 2003). The potential solar homeowner should consult their tax advisor to get the most current tax deduction and tax credit information for solar energy.

12.3   PAYBACK ANALYSIS

An example payback analysis would be helpful to the reader to see how these solar incentive programs help encourage solar designs. The Berkeley solar house can be used as an example assuming it was constructed today.

The first step is to list the solar equipment items and their capital costs:

Heliodyne Gobi solar thermal collectors, 8 @ $800	= $ 6400
Piping, pump, solar controller	= $ 1500
ASE Americas solar PV collectors, 6 @ $1187	= $ 7123
Trace engineering, Model 4048UPV Inverter	= $ 2500
Electrical conduit, breaker, boxes, wires	= $ 1500
Hot water heater 120 gallons	= $ 1500
Controller and electrical backup heater	= $ 650
Heat pump heating/cooling	= $ 5500
Radiant floor coils and valves	= $ 6500
Air cooling coils, ducting, dampers	= $ 5700
Fans, 3	= $ 1200
Automatic Smart house touch screen controller	= $ 26,945
Total capital cost	= **$ 67,018**

Next, installation labor is listed, which was greatly reduced by the fact that the roof was already sloped at 45° and only needed a stainless bracket under the tile to support the rails, on which the PV collectors were mounted:

Solar PV collectors, inverter, and wiring	= $ 2300
Solar thermal collectors	= $ 2500
Miscellaneous	= $ 1000
Total labor cost	= **$ 5800**

Next, the credits are listed:

State solar PV Buy-down Program, $3.50 @ 1.8 kW$_{peak}$	= $ 6300
Solar thermal state tax deduction	= $ 5500
Federal solar tax credit	= $ 5000
Total tax credits	= **$ 16,800**

Now, the annual heat/cooling cost savings plus electrical usage are listed for a non-solar house in the Berkeley hills area with a swimming pool:

Space heating for house, 1150 therms @ $1.25	= $ 1437
Swimming pool heating, 2300 therms @ $1.25	= $ 2875
Swimming pool filter pump, 1440 kWh @ 13¢/kWh	= $ 187
Space heat pump cooling, 7000 kWh @ 13¢/kWh	= $ 910
Domestic hot water, 1100 therms @ $1.25	= $ 1375
Electrical consumption, 200 m² @ 40 kWh/m² @ 13¢/kWh	= $ 1040
Total annual energy savings	= **$ 7824**

The simple payback in years is calculated by taking the capital cost of the extra solar equipment used in the solar house minus the one time tax credits divided by the annual energy savings over a conventional house in the area:

$$\text{Simple payback} = (\$67{,}018 + \$5800 - \$16{,}800)/\$7824$$
$$= 7.16 \text{ years}$$

By comparison, consider the case where there is only the solar PV Buy-down Program and no other tax credits, the simple payback would be:

$$\text{Simple payback} = (\$67{,}018 + \$5800 - \$6300)/\$7824$$
$$= 8.50 \text{ years}$$

This is particularly attractive when you consider that this covers the range of 12–14% return on investment in a decade where the stock market has not been able to return 10% interest on your investment.

Consider the case of a solar house with the same solar equipment but no swimming pool, then it would be:

$$\text{Simple payback} = (\$67{,}018 + \$5800 - \$6300)/\$4762$$
$$= 13.9 \text{ years}$$

This is around 7.2% return on investment and still attractive compared to investment into a CD or bond with very little risk.

The conclusion any potential homeowner will come to from looking at the economics today around the world is that solar houses are attractive financially, with typically an 8-year payback. And when the personal pleasure and satisfaction from living a solar life is also added, and knowing the positive effect on the environment and energy conservation influence on their friends, the personal payback is even more significant.

ENDNOTE

1. Solar Buy-down program, www.consumerenergycenter.org

13

Thermal performance monitoring and control

13.1 Real-time data display
13.2 Archiving data
13.3 Analyzing data trends
13.4 Scheduling
13.5 Adaptive controls
13.6 Optimization
13.7 Interface with other automated control functions

13.1 REAL-TIME DATA DISPLAY

The operation of the solar house involves an interaction with its occupants. This is done through the real-time display of location temperatures, system functions, and modes of operations. It can be done by standing right at the touch screen and touch-opening the pages desired: display of house temperatures, Schedule, Mechanical (systems diagrams), Trends, etc. Or it can be done by dialing in from a remote computer or personal digital assistant (PDA), and opening up a duplicate copy of the touch screen through the browser. From the browser, real-time actions can be carried out with the mouse cursor to fully operate the system remotely.

It is very helpful to see the entire view of the house and the temperatures throughout. One can see the rooms that are hot, the ones that are cool, and the control modes that are in operation. One can also change the heating or cooling setpoints for any of the spaces and can change the trigger points for any of the modes. For example, one could change greenhouse heating from being triggered at 18.3°C (65°F) up to 20°C (68°F) and many other combinations. The priority order can be fixed for the modes coming first and the ones coming last. These priorities can be changed with summer or winter seasons and be tuned or optimized based on past experience.

Having a real-time display showing all of these solar house temperatures and solar heating/cooling modes is very valuable, and after having lived with this capability, the homeowner could never live without this awareness of what is happening inside the solar house at any moment.

13.2   ARCHIVING DATA

An important responsibility of a solar homeowner is to communicate to others about the solar house to get many interested, to better understand its operation, and to constantly improve its operation throughout the year, with all the impacts of different weather types and activities within the house.

A necessary component of these responsibilities is to record temperatures in the living spaces and other systems operational data while the systems are working. This is termed "Thermal Performance Monitoring". This could be done by hand, but it is far easier to have this done as part of the building control system. In the case of the Berkeley house, the real-time logging of data and the charting of data trends were done as part of the Invensys hardware using the language called "Niagara," by Tridium, Inc. In this software language, there are many functions involving logging of data, such as in Table 13.1.

Table 13.1   Functions involving logging of data.

Application routine needed	Niagara object used
• Logging or trending of any:	
— Floating point value	AnalogLog
— Boolean state (On/Off, etc.)	BinaryLog
— Integer value	IntegerLog
— Multi-state value (Off/On/Fast, etc.)	MultistateLog
— String (alphanumeric text, or results of most any type output)	StringLog
• Holiday definitions	Calendar
• Scheduling control	Schedule
• Search and replace routine for property values in the stations database	AdminTool
• Any custom application routine or control function routine not available by using other application objects or standard control objects	Program

13.3   ANALYZING DATA TRENDS

An understanding of the important physical phenomena affecting the performance of your solar house is greatly enhanced by the use of a powerful graphical data plotting package that displays the on-going data trends.

In the high-end control systems software, such as by Invensys Energy Solutions (Invensys, 2003) that was used in the Berkeley house, there is a powerful trending package included. A variety of temperature and other sensors signals are linked to the module called AnalogLog which dutifully captures the data on the fly and stores it for plotting when requested by the user. On the color-touch screen, at the upper right, there are three touch-buttons: Schedule, Mechanical, Trends, as shown in Figure 13.1. When the "trends" button area is touched, a list of sensors are displayed, from which the desired sensors can be selected for plotting. When this is done and "chart" is touched, a plot is displayed instantly, as illustrated in Figure 13.2. Such a chart shows

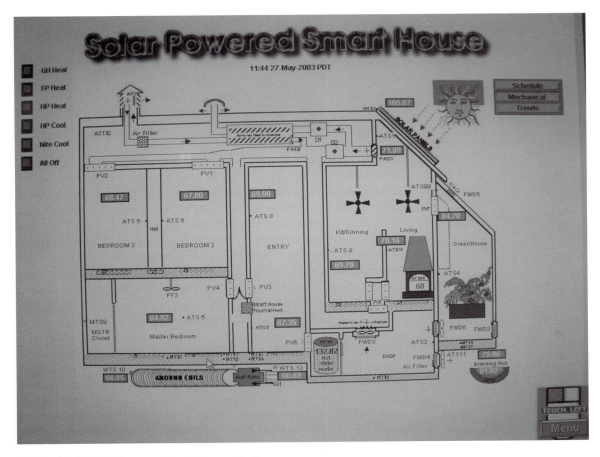

Figure 13.1   Touch screen trending analysis.

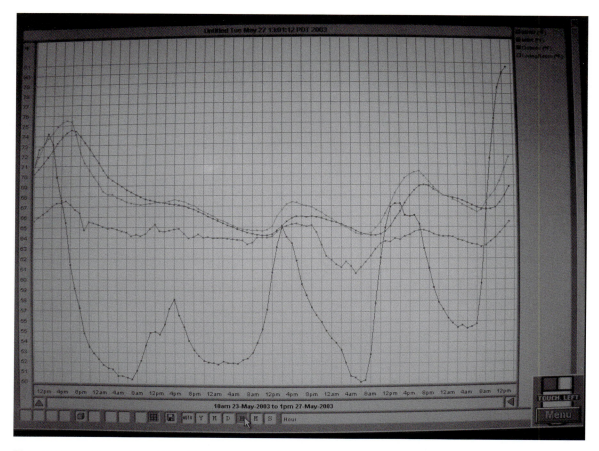

Figure 13.2   Example temperature plot for trending analysis.

the values of the sensors, such as temperatures versus time and date from the time when data logging started as far back as 6 months, or whatever time interval selected. If there are more than 6 months of data, the data older than 6 months is dropped off and only the last 6 months displayed. If there is a particular region of the plot that needs to be enlarged for detailed study, this can be done by simply touching and dragging the area to enlarge that portion of the plot.

One can display such plots showing a number of temperature locations, such as outside, living room, master bed room, upstairs, solar panels, ground-source underground coils, heat pump output, swimming pool, greenhouse, etc. On one plot, as many of these particular temperatures can be selected for plotting on the same plot, so one can examine the relationship between sensors and their variation with time. We showed a number of examples in the previous chapters. But having this real-time and on-line for instant examination is incredibly valuable. The example shown in Figure 13.2 reveals how rapidly the downstairs and upstairs temperatures drop during the nighttime using the nocturnal cooling mode. A short experiment therein was done by opening an MBR window to see the momentary drop in MBR temperature over one hour. After this drop, the window was closed to observe the return to previous temperature, owing to the storage of heat from the thermal mass.

It is possible to study temperature response of the ground coils to heating or cooling modes, radiant floor heating coil use to maintain temperatures of any zone, the swimming pool temperature change over season or how rapidly it heats on a hot day or cools over a period of several cold foggy days. One can also examine how greenhouse temperature affects various types of vegetables or watering cycle and many other intriguing phenomena that occur inside and around the solar house.

It allows selection of two different types of sensors, such as temperature and power load. The trending software will plot both results with a dual y-axis: one for temperature and one for kilowatts. This allows one to analyze the relationship with temperature events and power consumed (or produced). This is important for doing optimization using energy management, as described in Section 13.6.

One can also gather binary information, via BinaryLog, where events, such as heat pump turned on/off, ceiling fan turned on/off, solar thermal collector pumps turned on/off, etc., and also to study the relationship of temperature changes against any or a combination of these control events.

Of course, these plots can be saved in a file and then downloaded for further numerical analysis with common programs such as Microsoft Excel, etc.

This short description is just a portion of what is possible with trending analysis capability, and the solar homeowner should strongly insist that such a feature be an integral part of their solar control system.

13.4   SCHEDULING

There should be a scheduling capability to change the regular control systems operation according to a daily, weekly, or a monthly plan. The Invensys (Niagara operating system) control system used in the Berkeley house, has this capability and it is very powerful. The following provides an overview of some of the features of this scheduling system.

Figure 13.3 shows a weekly schedule that is used where the system is active and running everyday of the week for 24 hours of the day. For such a schedule, all hours of every day are shaded. If one selects certain hours of a day or certain

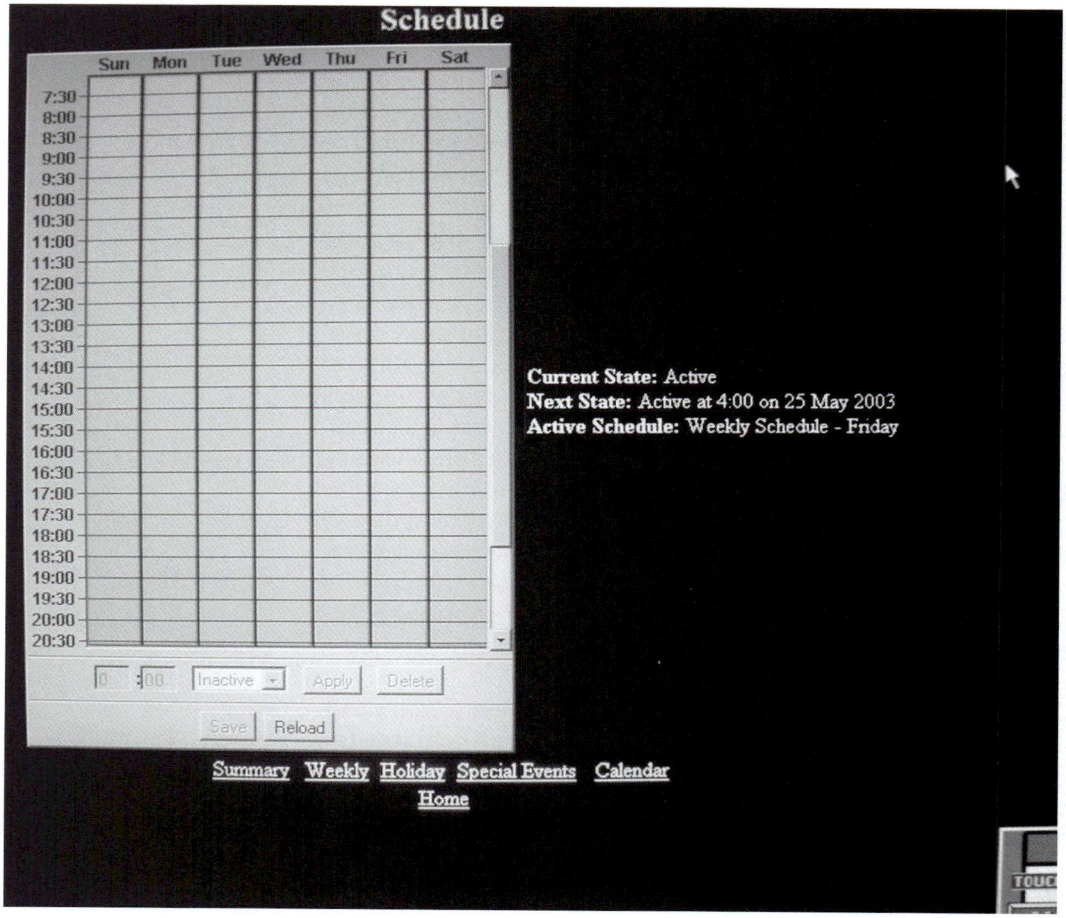

Figure 13.3   Weekly scheduling.

days (such as weekend), the selected hours can be unshaded so that the system goes to an inactive state, or a state that the homeowner can define. Such a special "away" operation, may involve changing set-points by setting back the heating temperature set-points to lower values and the cooling set-points to higher values to save energy.

For situations where the homeowner is away for a trip and knows the return date and time, the system can be scheduled to turn on again so that the solar home will be at the desired temperature upon the homeowners' arrival.

Scheduling beyond a week can be handled by a monthly schedule, as shown in Figure 13.4, and a number of monthly schedules. The months can be scrolled forward or backward through the touch screen.

Special events can also be programmed into the scheduling function, and this feature is enormously powerful. For example,

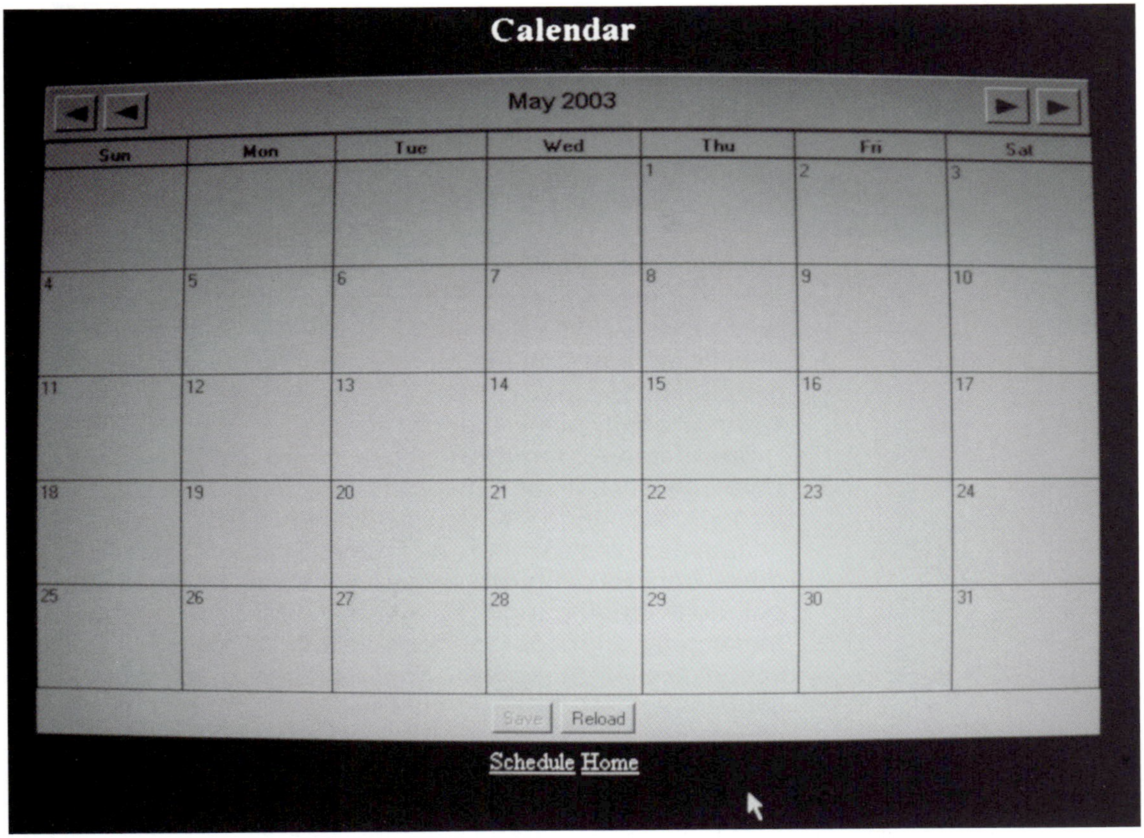

Figure 13.4   Monthly calendar scheduling.

a number of special events can be defined and selected to go into effect at any time or date of any month over a year, or can be scheduled to be repeated at regular intervals, such as every Friday, or every 2nd Wednesday, or whatever.

These special events, when triggered according to the schedule, involve sending a binary integer into the control system logic, where different set-points can be triggered, different modes of operation, different priority of modes, etc.

In fact, this scheduling capability allows one to do either adaptive or optimization of the solar home operation according to long-term weather predictions, which are getting better and more reliable every year. Suppose, for instance, one knows that a cold weather front will be arriving at the solar home site on a particular day. Using the scheduling capability, one can change the set-points to increase the house to higher temperatures using the solar heating available to store more heat in the thermal mass within the house and carry further into the coming colder days. The reverse can be done when an approaching warm weather front is predicted. This kind of scheduling has been done for the Berkeley house, and it is very effective in accomplishing the desired temperatures for a longer period of time while saving substantial quantities of energy.

13.5   ADAPTIVE CONTROLS

There are just a few adaptive controls in the market, such as learning thermostats or learning occupancy sensors (that turn lights on when someone comes into the room and off after they leave, HomeControls, 2003). But these are very simple and are not interactive and do not work together to carryout sophisticated control actions.

So, adaptive controls are those controls that get better and more efficient at automatically operating the solar house through "learning" the strategy that works best. One way these adaptive controls work is by "remembering" everything one does with the control system, whether be changing set-points, overriding mode changes, etc. This can also be done by keeping a logbook of one's actions in response to some action taken by the control system and informing their control contractor to add these "little tweaks" to the control logic. Of course, the control system that has been described in this book allows for the control contractor to dial in, make the changes, and sign off. The author had done this for about 4 months and the control logic improvements usually take only a few minutes to add. It only requires a phone call to explain the observation, and the contractor takes over from this point and has the improved control code running in a very short time.

Although not part of the Berkeley house, true adaptive controls are being "tuned" and improved behind the scenes and frequently use "neural networks." This is a scheme that "learns" much like the human brain by making connections and memorizing through the association of facts or actions. For example, in dry summer weather the homeowner may find the air conditioning set-point higher than 22°C (72°F) which triggers the heat-pump chiller operation. So the system learns to increase the set-point in the middle of summer when it is dry.

Another example of adaptive control is to utilize measurements of wind direction, intensity, humidity, temperature, and barometer to predict in advance an approaching cold fog cycle and to allow the house to increase in temperature above the normal set-points in order to carry stored heat for many days through this fog cycle and avoid triggering mechanical heating. Likewise, weather predictions of a cold front or warm front from the web can be used to change the solar house control system dynamics. And the true adaptive control systems will learn how well these predictions worked and adjust itself accordingly to improve the performance of the solar house. Using one's own vision and creativity will allow them to devise new and better ways to use adaptive control.

13.6   OPTIMIZATION

Optimization of the control system is similar to adaptive controls, but there is an objective function or objective measure that is used to decide if the control system change is better or worse. Consider the objective function of electricity use. It may well turn out that operating the fans for 8 hours in nocturnal cooling mode be may slightly excessive when one considers the cost of electricity off-peak. So this is a balance between getting the house just a little cooler before the start of the next day versus using more electric energy off-peak.

Energy management

This important optimization is perhaps the most important for the solar homeowner. In the Berkeley house, there is the task of simultaneously managing both the solar thermal energy collected and the solar PV-generated electricity. These are complex and challenging tasks that can be left to the automatic controls or to the homeowner trying to constantly improve over the obvious control actions. One important sensor that makes this possible is the current sensor or current toroid (CT), which consists of a small, inexpensive coil placed around a wire running between the energy source and the energy consuming device. Figure 13.5 shows a CT device.

Now as an example, the two most important CT locations are (1) between the solar PV inverter output and the main electrical power distribution panel and (2) at the utility meter. This will reveal the solar PV current output into the house and the current going back to the utility for credit or being pulled from utility to supply the house. For more detailed examination of real-time energy use, these CTs can be placed on each significant sub-branch of the electrical distribution panel in the house to reveal energy use in each living area: kitchen, laundry, entertainment area, home office, shop, etc.

From these CTs, one can calculate the power consumption of the house as well as the solar PV electrical power fed back into the grid for credit. This information permits energy optimization of the house to be accomplished. It is truly amazing to know how much energy can be saved when the homeowner has the energy information displayed conveniently and in real-time to help in making energy utilization choices.

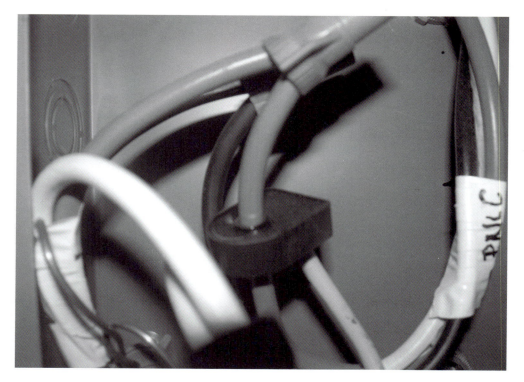

Figure 13.5   The current Toroid sensor.

Now one can add to this picture the information from the utility, that the electricity costs 31.5¢/kWh during peak energy periods of weekdays noon to 6 pm; otherwise it costs only 9.5¢/kWh. This would apply to the homeowner if the Time-Of-Use (TOU) Net-Metering billing option is selected from the utility. If this is not selected, then electricity use is billed at the levelized rate of 13¢/kWh. This is a difficult choice indeed, and the use of TOU Net-Metering can create large savings only if the solar home has a program of active energy management. These savings are important in paying back the initial capital investment in solar equipment for the solar house. Also it is important to note, as discussed in Chapter 12, that with active energy management and various financial rebates and tax deductions, the solar house investment can indeed payback very well and represent a great investment.

13.7   INTERFACE WITH OTHER AUTOMATED CONTROL FUNCTIONS

There are times when the solar homeowner prefers interactions between the solar automatic controls and other automated functions such as lighting. In Figure 13.6 is shown the typical

Figure 13.6 Interaction with lighting functions.

Levitron* multi-light function switch. This lighting control switch uses the X-10® method of using the power line to send control signals that turn on and off lights anywhere in the house. These pushbuttons are back-illuminated to show their labels and to show the lights which are actually turned on. Although it is beyond the subject of this book, there is a whole subject of power line carrier devices that will turn on lights, outlets, appliances, etc., detect that they have turned on and send a confirming signal back to the local switch. There are also dimming functions, pre-programmed light illumination scenes, etc. The homeowner will find subtle incentives for interactions between lighting scene controls and thermal and ventilation control.

In addition to lighting, when the homeowner wants to override or alter temporarily the HVAC automatic controls, the "push on-push off", toggle switch panels that are placed strategically in the solar house are used. The largest one is located in the master bedroom, as shown in Figure 13.7. There are six push buttons in this panel to cover a range of selections needed to be made in the master bedroom. These push buttons are back-lighted to show that this selection is on and to illuminate the label in the dark as shown in Figure 13.8. The dark dot is

*Levitron (2003), a company that manufactures a large range of electrical switches, outlets, boxes, etc. (www.Levitron.com).

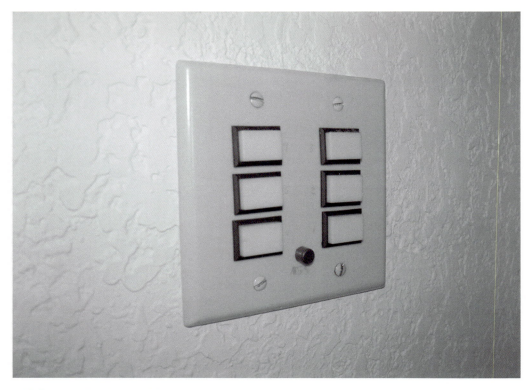

Figure 13.7   Localized special function toggle switches.

Figure 13.8   Backlighting toggle switches.

the local thermistor sensor that measures the local temperature at that point. These toggle switches are not available and had to be custom-designed and assembled by the homeowner. They interact with the Invensys Niagara control system by providing a binary input, which the software detects and alters its operation as desired.

Anyone might want to know what special control-system overrides or local input the solar homeowner desires. A starting example is to interact with the ceiling fan system at a large dinner party, where the fans may need to be increased or decreased in speed. It should be noted that birthday cake candles are sensitive to air flow, etc. There may be instances when the fan operation has to be temporarily stopped during a telephone call for hearing very faint conversations. The homeowner may want to set up a particular lighting scene for a dinner party during eating, a lowered illumination after dinner, and a different one for cleaning up after the dinner. There are also times when one might want a certain outdoor lighting scene when guests arrive and while going to their cars for departure. There are also outdoor evening barbeques, swim parties, dancing, etc. There are lighting scenes that may be needed for X-mas decorations.

There is the topic of the Home Wide Web – a wired network backbone that provides an interface and communication with major appliances in the home. An excellent summary of the current status of "smart appliances" is given in Electronic House (www.electronichouse.com). The network is based on "Internet Protocol" or IP control. It is like having one's own Internet – or Intranet. Appliances and other devices have their own webpages that come up so one can talk to each of them and tell them what they want them to do and when. The appliances have a Ethernet chip inside with a RJ45 connector (looks like a wide phone connector). This RJ45 connector plugs into the wall where the IP network is interconnected with Cat 5e or Cat 6 wiring (looks like coax cable but with a particular rating for this IP service). For new constructions, it would be wise to wire up such outlets and be prepared for the exciting new smart appliances that are just beginning to appear. The latest systems are using wireless pocket PCs that talk directly to this network from any room, outside, and even from the car for up to 1000 ft. It is certainly exciting, so one can look for these new smart appliances and plan to wire with Cat 6 wiring every chance they get.

There is also the huge topic of entertainment systems control. This topic is beyond the subject of this book, but the reader should be aware that there are multi-room sound systems, outdoor audio programming, control of sound sources from remote rooms and outside. There are times when a phone call requires temporary muting of the speaker systems so that the caller can be heard. The creative homeowner can imagine many more such custom functions.

14

Solar energy future options

14.1   FUTURE DEVELOPMENTS

At least three new areas of development are expected to greatly enhance the capabilities of the solar house (and commercial buildings too).

Building integrated PV collectors

From the positive experience of the Berkeley house with greenhouse/sunroom kits available today that will now accept dual-glazed heat mirror glazing, one can find that the large all-glass and sealed ASE Americas collectors will work in these kits as well. So, now there is a combined use for the PV collector – as a sealed roof element, as a PV electric source, and as a source of heat. They are nearly opaque except for the regular matrix of checkerboard spaces around the silicon crystal sections laminated between the glass elements. However, the amount of clear openings is variable to some degree and can be a planned architectural feature. Also some of the amorphous solar collector materials are partially transparent over their entire surface. If these kits are used for the house roof or wall structure and not a greenhouse/sunroom function, then the PV collector opacity is not of concern. Heating of air is possible beneath these PV collectors, mounted and sealed in this way. In addition, in this hot air plenum, the electrical connections to the PV collector can be made easily.

Figure 14.1   Powerlight foam solar PV collector roof tiles.

The combined PV collector integrated into the roof or wall has an improved economic payback from amortization as a roof member as well as generating heat and electricity.

A well-known example of roof-integrated solar PV collectors are made by Powerlight (2003), where they use tongue and groove-interlocked foam tiles on top of which is mounted the solar PV collector section. These foam tiles cover the unshaded portion of a nearly horizontal roof without any roof penetrations. The entire array is heavy enough and all interconnected so that they are safe from wind damage. The foam covering on the roof provides extra insulation on the roof that reduces heating costs in winter and air conditioning costs in summer. This PV collector system covering over a standard tar and gravel roof greatly extends the life of the roof, saving long-term roofing costs. Figure 14.1 shows such an installation at the Chabot Space and Science Center in Oakland, California. The same Powerlight product can be used on residential roofs if they are slightly sloped. Most of their installations are for light commercial buildings.

Combined solar PV and thermal collectors

A combined solar PV and thermal collector (PVT) is shown in Figure 14.2 and it has been discussed in some detail in

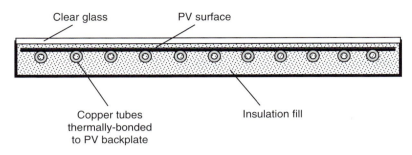

Figure 14.2   Cross-section of a solar PVT collector.

Chapter 6. The collector looks just like a solar thermal collector with a glazing front cover and a heat-absorbing backplate below the glass with thermally-bonded copper tubes affixed to the back of the plate. The glycol flows through the tubes and extracts the heat from this collector. In the PVT collector, the backplate is replaced with the PV surface that generates electricity. As discussed earlier, cooling the PV collector greatly improves the insolation to electricity output efficiency. In crystalline PV collectors, there is typically 0.5% improvement for each centigrade cooled, as the author measured. Using the ASE Americas (model DG 300/60) a clear sunny day produced collector temperatures of 50°C (122°F) resulting in a PV collector efficiency of 8.35%. The specifications for this collector model indicate 0.50% increase in efficiency for every centigrade it cooled. For example, when the collector was cooled to 20°C (68°F) the efficiency increased to 13.39% – nearly double! So there is a huge incentive for actively cooling these PV collectors in a combined design PVT collector.

An upgrade on the Berkeley house is being planned in another 10 years, as the existing thermal and PV collectors reach their 50% life-cycle point. At this option, a commercial PVT would be installed, such as now, being tested at full-scale in two beta test sites. There would be 14 collectors at 4.2 kW$_{peak}$ operating at fully realized efficiency of 15%. This efficiency is higher because the collector is cooled (see discussion about PV temperature effects in Chapter 6). The installed wiring and inverter were already sized for 5 kW$_{peak}$. The collector area would be 43 m^2 (448 ft^2) and would produce 22.4 kWh/day during sunny days or 5.3 MWh/year. As seen in earlier chapters the Berkeley house uses about 2.4 MWh/year. So this system not only provides all the electricity and heating needed for the house but also generates an income stream from the sale during noon to 6 pm of peak power at 32¢/kWh under new California State "Time-of-Use (TOU) Net Metering laws," requiring the local utility to buy in return such renewable energy so generated at the prescribed rate. This would be an income stream of $768/year after eliminating normal electricity and natural gas cost used by a typical house without solar system. The expected cost of these 14 PVT collectors is $4/$W_{peak}$ or $16,000, plus about $1000 for the simple installation of replacing the old ones with the new ones for a total of $17,000 as the solar system increment cost. By contrast, before solar, $160\,m^2$ ($1868\,ft^2$) house using $200\,kWh/m^2$ per year with needs of DHW, space heating, pool heating, and electricity had an energy bill of about $3500 per year for electricity plus $1500 per year for gas-heating the swimming pool or $5000 per year for total energy. Thus, since the savings with solar would be $5768/year, there would be a 2.94-year payback taking credit for the State Solar Buy-down Program. This program involves a rebate of either $4.50/$W_{peak}$ or 50% of the capital cost rebate, whichever is less, for a credit against the collector purchase totaling $8500 in this case. This improves the payback period to less than one year. In addition, Federal income tax deductions are also likely, which is a great incremental investment.

The case of installing such a system on a bare house without the advantage of having a previous separate thermal and PV collector system will now be examined. In this case, there would be the additional cost of roof-mounting hardware, roof installation, running wiring from the roof down to the inverter, a new 5 kW Xantrex Sunline inverter and the auxiliary cutoff switches as the utility may require. Updating the earlier actual out-of-pocket cost of $5000 in 2012 we expect $7000. So the new system would cost $24,000 for 14 PVT collectors, $4000 for inverter and electrical parts, and $7000 for installation, totaling $35,000. This would generate a rebate credit of $4.50/$W_{peak}$ for 4.2 kW_{peak} of $18,900. This cost is reduced to $16,100 after rebate cost. The total energy savings over the non-solar house would be $5768/year; thus, this solar project would have a payback of 2.8 years. This would be reduced somewhat after the expected Federal tax credit, which is still a great investment.

What makes these two PVT solar projects so incredibly attractive is that, the solar system is handling the entire energy load for the house plus a swimming pool operation, which typically triples a house's energy costs in electricity for filtering, chlorination pumps, and gas heating. In addition, a combined solar system with the electrical output properly sized to produce electrical power during peak period, eliminates the peak power load during noon to 6 pm, when electricity under TOU is most expensive, plus generates a small income stream. There is clearly an optimum sizing of the system as determined by detailed economic modeling covering the complex utility TOU net-metering billing rate structure. It is strongly suggested that the future solar homeowner, designer, and contractor take all of this into account when planning a solar home. This certainly is the time for considering solar PVT.

Fuel cells

Great advances are being made on fuel cells around the world (www.fuelcelltoday.com). Natural gas-powered fuel cells for homes are now being marketed internationally by Plug Power (www.plugpower.com). Some also work on propane. There is an attractive market for these fuel cells for the off-grid solar house. When the sun is not shining nor available to produce PV electricity and solar heat, the fuel cell can produce electric power and supply heat for hot water and space heating. The fuel cells provide a welcome alternative to the troublesome and expensive storage batteries required for off-grid solar houses assuming natural gas or propane is available.

There are new reversible fuel cells now being introduced that provide a wonderful synergy between the fuel cell and the off-grid solar house. What is so exciting is that, these fuel cells can be fed electric power from the solar PV, and they generate hydrogen gas, which can be stored on-site and reused in the fuel cell when the sun is not shining. A single reversible fuel cell can replace a pair of water electrolyzer and a conventional fuel cell, which together perform the hydrogen-regeneration function. The reversible fuel cell (manufactured by Proton Energy Systems, www.protonenergy.com) is only slightly more expensive than the standard fuel cell by Plug Power (2003), and in this way opens a new attractive market for solar houses, whether they are off-grid or grid-tied. As central fossil fuel-fired electric generating plants become more expensive, more unreliable and environmentally undesirable, solar hydrogen-regenerative fuel cell alternative will begin entering the grid-tied marketplace. Retrofits for the huge stock of existing houses, in regions of the world where the solar PV is particularly more attractive, are available and preferred over polluting fossil-fired plants. This ability to offer solar PV-produced electricity without batteries will be one more incentive for the solar house supplying both electricity and heat that is reliable, cost-effective, and not greenhouse gas-polluting.

Energy from waste for houses

The hydrogen-generation (Hygen) market has to be with the early adopters who can see the value in producing energy from their on-site generated waste. This energy from waste systems use natural gas as a backup only to augment any waste shortfall. The Plug Power front-end reformer can be a way to get started, but buyers should be aware that huge increases in natural gas prices are likely within 3–4 years.

Figure 14.3 shows the front end of a small-scale steam reformer that converts waste into hydrogen-rich syngas. Although the author has designed and built prototype commercial units for waste conversion, they are not yet available in the marketplace for residences.

So fuel cells converting the energy in the hydrogen feedstream to heat and electrical energy should be noted. With fuel cells of today, half the feedstock energy is used to drive the fuel cell to produce electricity at 50% efficiency, while the remaining 50% can generate heat.

A check on the waste quantity to supply a home's energy needs can be done assuming 1 ton/person-year (Curlee, 1994)

Figure 14.3 Residential prototype steam reforming of waste.

of general garbage including sewage solid waste plus about 5 tons/year per household for green yard waste. If 5 persons/household were assumed, the total is 10 tons/year per household. So it can be assumed that this makes 10 tons/year of syngas (see Glossary) or 4.8 kWh/kg (7500 Btu/lb at 300 Btu/dscf with a density of 0.04 lb/dscf) or 22 MWh/year (75,000 MBtu/yr). (A sanity check for municipal solid waste (MSW) shows its heating value as 3.9 kWh/kg (6000 Btu/lb) in an inefficient furnace). With 50% electricity by the fuel cell and 50% heat for the building, the electricity would be 11,000 kWh/year and the thermal energy would be the same number. This is more than the most inefficient houses consume. For example, the Berkeley house with a pool uses only 2400 kWh/year electricity.

A check can be made also on space heating requirements of a house. An efficient European house needs 15–30 kWh/m^2-yr. So a 150 m^2 house in Europe will consume 2250–4500 kW/year (7–15,000 MBtu/yr). Therefore, in this energy from waste scheme, it is possible to generate more thermal energy than is used in an efficient house for space heating.

Now consider using this extra thermal energy to steam reform the waste to produce hydrogen for vehicles. Assuming they are driving 8000 km/year (5000 miles/yr at 20 mpg gasoline base) that is 950 L of petrol/year (250 gal of gasoline/yr). With gasoline at 9.63 kWh/L (125,000 Btu/gal), this is 9.6 MWh/year (33,000 MBtu/yr) – comparable to the number calculated above at 11,000 kWh/year (75,000 MBtu/yr) as the extra heat available from waste. This generates enough hydrogen providing the same amount of energy to the vehicle as gasoline, which shows that the concept can work to use the extra heat to steam reform waste into hydrogen on-site.

So in conclusion, this is really a pretty good match all around. So why aren't we considering local energy from waste more seriously?

The price could be worked out by going backward and assuming that the system has to pay for itself through savings over, say, 15 years. The fuel cell qualifies for $4500/kWh rebate or 50% of the capital cost of the equipment, which ever is less, through the California Energy Commission Buy-down program. Only fuel cells that use renewable fuel qualify for this rebate. There is also a Federal Tax credit for fuel cells used in homes. Though the author has not developed a detailed design for costing, it is crudely guessed that $50,000 budget would work for a 2.5 kWe fuel cell – steam reformer system. So the rebate is $11,250 and assuming the IRS tax credit to be 25% or $12,500, the balance of $26,250 is amortized over

15 years or $3500/year interest plus principal. The savings in electricity of 2.5 kWh/h is $2847/year at 13¢/kWh and in heating of 4.4 MWh/year (15,000 MBtu/yr at 60¢/therm) is $900/year, which totals to $3747/year. Garbage, plastics, paper, and yard waste bills are eliminated at about $300/year. So there is a saving of about $4047/year, which would payback the initial investment plus interest in less than 15 years. So even the economics work out.

Now the question is, can this waste steam reformer be built for $50,000–60,000 retail price? Not sure precisely, but it is a great business goal for a future technology high volume business.

14.2   ROLE OF RENEWABLES IN THE GLOBAL ENERGY FUTURE

In the US during of 1973–1984, the sudden increase in energy costs triggered a greater attention to energy management in buildings, from residential to commercial. As a result of this consciousness, buildings greatly improved in energy efficiency in aspects such as wall insulation, improved window design, improved heating and cooling systems, etc. There were typically 40% improvements in the energy efficiency of commercial buildings (Solar Energy Research Institute, 1988, pg. 9) to an annual 126 kWh/m^2 (40 kBtu/ft^2) and a similar improvement in new or rebuilt residential buildings to an annual 25 kWh/m^2 (8 kBtu/ft^2). These statistics documenting the substantial improvement in energy efficiency of buildings make it possible for solar houses to now become technically and economically feasible.

From the example given in Section 14.1 it can be seen that renewables such as solar and waste streams can, in fact, supply the energy demands of a solar house plus a renewable hydrogen fuel cell hybrid vehicle. This use of residential solar thermal and PV plus waste is a significant portion of the renewable energy growth curve shown in Figures 1.1 and 1.2. The solar thermal and PV industry growth is somewhere between 26% and 43% per year and the solar house is an important contribution one can make today to continue to follow along this important renewables growth curve in Figure 1.1.

Figure 14.4 shows how all these various technologies converting solar and wind energy into hydrogen can fit together and how the hydrogen can be used to power an entire community of the future, not depending on fossil fuels. Solar and wind can usher in the "Hydrogen Economy" (Rifkin, 2002) even on a local resident basis, discussed in the following sections.

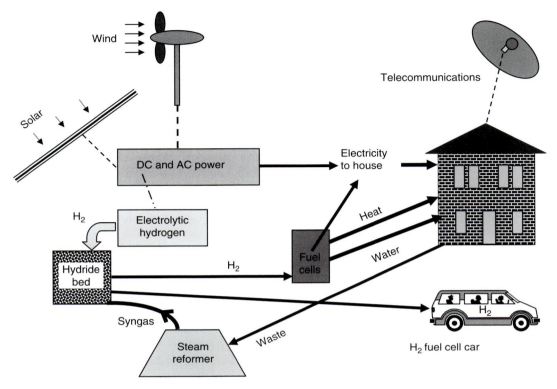

Figure 14.4 Diagram of the hydrogen economy.

14.3 WIND/SOLAR HYBRID SYNERGIES

Another entire subject is the generation of energy from wind, which is beyond the scope of this book. An excellent compact summary of the technology and engineering design basis has been given (Kreith and Kreider, 1978, pg. 577–600). A current summary of the global impact of wind energy has been given (EUREC, 2002, pg. 138–172). The average annual growth rate of this wind generator industry has been 31%. Europe hosts 74% or 13,630 MW of the world's wind capacity that totals 18,449 MW. About 10,000 MW of this installed capacity includes small, grid-tied wind generators in the <10 kW size range for individual houses. Interestingly, these small-sized generators had been used since the mid-1800s on small farms for water pumping and small DC power loads. Now there is resurgence and this new market is starting to grow (EUREC, 2002, 149 pp). Contrastingly, the estimated global installed base of solar PV at the end of 2002 is about 2100 MW with last year's annual production of PV collectors at 360 MW. Now one can see there is an exciting opportunity for combined wind and solar in homes.

There is a strong incentive for the combined wind and solar systems in homes because of the unique synergy between the two very different technologies. The synergy derives from the nature of day/night cycle and the weather. Wind continues to blow at night, whereas there is no sunlight at night for solar thermal or PV. During cloudy/rainy weather there are often strong winds when there is no solar available. In strong storm fronts, there are strong winds but long periods of up to one week without any sun. By contrast during calm sunny days, there is strong solar energy but little wind. Thus this synergy holds very well over a wide range of weather conditions.

The small wind turbines have rotor diameters of only 0.5–1.5 m (1.5–4.5 ft) and are very quiet with noise levels well below 40 db. Being small, they can be mounted on a small stand on the roof in an unobstructed windy location. For homes, the small size is normally allowed under zoning and code ordinances. The cost for these small-size units (Whisper H40), easily roof pipe-mounted by homeowners, is about $1600 for supplying about 200 kWh per month in a 7.2 m/s (16 mph) wind (Jade Mountain, 2002). The voltage range can be selected so that they can be added to an existing solar PV inverter for a grid-tied system without batteries. This is a very cost-effective system producing power at about 15¢/kWh for a 9-year payback with a 50% wind factor.

14.4   VEHICLES POWERED BY ELECTROLYTIC HYDROGEN

Using solar PV and/or wind to generate hydrogen for hydrogen fuel cell-hybrid vehicles is an exciting new area that has worldwide appeal and support. The reversible fuel cell is a technology that can accept electrical power and electrolyze water to make high purity hydrogen gas under pressure. This hydrogen is compressed into tanks in the fuel cell-hybrid vehicle to provide enough energy onboard for an extended driving range. Proton Energy Systems estimate (corporate stock prospectus underwritten by Lehman Brothers) that the hydrogen-powered vehicle production will quickly ramp up from 750 vehicles in 2004 to 25,000 in 2007 and to 1 million vehicles in 2010. Their systems are initially aimed at the community-fuel station market, but small systems would be a possible market for individual homes with solar PV clean electricity available.

Another electrolytic hydrogen-generator supplier is Stuart Energy (www.stuartenergy.com), who is a world leader in supplying clean hydrogen fuel via water electrolysis for fuel cell vehicles and environmentally friendly energy applications. They have been building hydrogen electrolysis units since they were founded in 1948. On April 22, 2003, Toyota opened the first hydrogen fuel station in Southern California using the Stuart Energy system. Their newest system can supply hydrogen under pressures up to 10,000 psi for the Ford and other automobile company onboard fiber-wound hydrogen storage tanks. Figure 14.5 shows the author's Ford Focus, the model that Ford has announced will next be available commercially as a fuel cell hybrid. It can be supplied with hydrogen supplied from solar PV-generated electricity. The division of Stuart Energy that has been supplying the large-scale hydrogen electrolyzers used in the process industries is called "The Electrolyzer Corporation Ltd., also in Mississauga, Ontario, Canada.

So it is like witnessing a historical event – this is the beginning of the hydrogen economy as envisioned by Jeremy Rifkin (Rifkin, 2002) with hydrogen generated by renewable clean energy sources that are not dependent on fossil fuel in

Figure 14.5   Ford focus – the next solar fuel cell hybrid.

any manner; well introduced in his address to the European Union in Brussel on June 16–17, 2003:

Imagining a world without oil
Imagine, for a moment, a world where fossil fuels are no longer burned to generate power, heat and light. A world no longer threatened by global warming or geopolitical conflict in the Middle East. A world where every person on earth has access to electricity. That world now looms on the horizon.

We are in the early stages of an historic change in the way we organize the Earth's energy. The Industrial Age, which began with the carrying of coal from Newcastle several hundred years ago, is now winding down in the oil fields of the Middle East. Meanwhile, a wholly new energy regime is being readied. Hydrogen – the lightest and most abundant element of the universe – is the next great energy revolution. Scientists call it the "forever fuel" because it never runs out. And when hydrogen is used to produce power, the only byproducts are pure water and heat. Hydrogen has the potential to end the world's reliance on oil from the Persian Gulf, the most politically unstable and volatile region of the world. Indeed, making the transition to hydrogen is the best assurance against the prospects of future oil wars in the Middle East. Hydrogen will also dramatically cut down on carbon dioxide emissions and mitigate the effects of global warming. And because hydrogen is so plentiful, people who have never before had access to electricity will be able to generate it."

14.5   FUEL CELLS FOR ELECTRICITY AND HEAT

The best known residential fuel cell program underway in the US is by Plug Power (2003), a partnership with General Electric, who does the installation and service (www.plugpower.com). These fuel cells are based on a high temperature polymer membrane (PEM), and must use hydrogen obtained by reforming natural gas or propane on-site. The combination of reformer and fuel cell is about the size of a washer/dryer set and are frequently placed outside the house for hydrogen safety. As on date, Plug Power has 126 units installed, with a total of about a million operating hours, producing about 2650 MWh of electricity.

Their GenSys® models range from 2 to 25 kW, from residential to light commercial buildings. For example, the GenSys® model 5C produces 2.5 to 5 kW of electric power and 9 kW of thermal power simultaneously from a natural gas input. It produces voltage output of 120 V AC, 60 Hz as standard with an option for 208 V AC and 240 V AC. The unit is 2 m long × 0.9 m wide × 1.8 m high (74" long × 32" wide × 68.25" high) and designed for outside installation. It has product certifications by FCC as Class B, ANSI, CSA International, UL, and CE. The GenSys® model 5C public spec sheet is provided in Figure 14.6. It is believed that the pricing will be in the range of

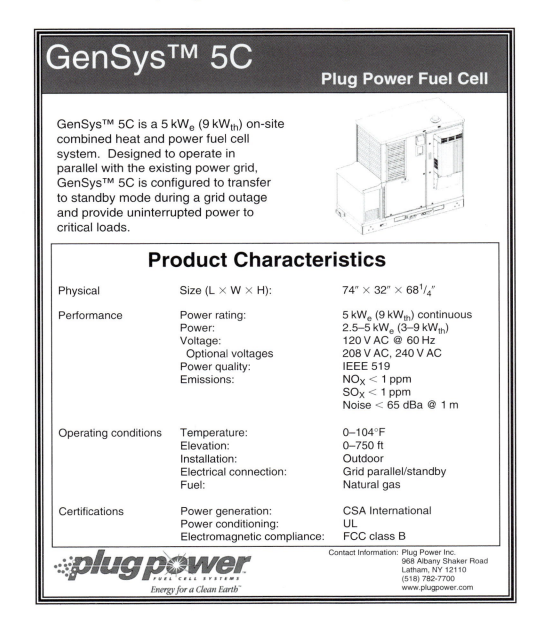

GenSys™ 5C
Plug Power Fuel Cell

GenSys™ 5C is a 5 kW$_e$ (9 kW$_{th}$) on-site combined heat and power fuel cell system. Designed to operate in parallel with the existing power grid, GenSys™ 5C is configured to transfer to standby mode during a grid outage and provide uninterrupted power to critical loads.

Product Characteristics

Physical	Size (L × W × H):	74" × 32" × 68$^{1}/_{4}$"
Performance	Power rating:	5 kW$_e$ (9 kW$_{th}$) continuous
	Power:	2.5–5 kW$_e$ (3–9 kW$_{th}$)
	Voltage:	120 V AC @ 60 Hz
	Optional voltages	208 V AC, 240 V AC
	Power quality:	IEEE 519
	Emissions:	NO$_X$ < 1 ppm
		SO$_X$ < 1 ppm
		Noise < 65 dBa @ 1 m
Operating conditions	Temperature:	0–104°F
	Elevation:	0–750 ft
	Installation:	Outdoor
	Electrical connection:	Grid parallel/standby
	Fuel:	Natural gas
Certifications	Power generation:	CSA International
	Power conditioning:	UL
	Electromagnetic compliance:	FCC class B

plug power
FUEL CELL SYSTEMS
Energy for a Clean Earth™

Contact Information: Plug Power Inc.
968 Albany Shaker Road
Latham, NY 12110
(518) 782-7700
www.plugpower.com

Figure 14.6   Plug Power spec sheet for residential fuel cell.

$30,000–66,000 depending on the details of the installation, quantity, etc. As on date, the GenSys 5C prime power fuel cell system is being sold for test and demonstration purposes to target customers in order to maximize their learning and to assist in the commercialization of the GenSys product family. The GenSys 5C is not ready right now for sale to the general public. It is typically placed with organizations such as utilities, national testing laboratories, universities, and certifying agencies. When the GenSys products contain the feature set required by the residential market, they will become available for sale to the general public. Their commercialization progress and product availability will be posted on the Plug Power website at www.plugpower.com. So it is worth watching this new company.

There is a powerful synergy between solar PV and natural gas or propane-powered fuel cells. These fuel cells will replace the need for batteries in off-grid installations. When there is no sunlight or inadequately low levels of sunlight, the fuel cell can produce the electricity and thermal energy. When there is enough sunlight for PV electricity and solar thermal for heating, the fuel cell can shutoff. There is a reasonable turn down of fuel cell output of around 50%, so that it can do a limited amount of load-following. As the residential and light commercial market begins to grow substantially, it is projected that the prices will drop substantially to $3000/kW or lower and the residential fuel cell market will take off.

References and Further reading

Adams, Robert W., (1981), "*Adding Solar Heat to Your Home*," Tab Books, Inc., PA, 280 pp.

ASE Americas, Inc., (1998), Product Literature, 4 Suburban Park Drive, Billerica, MA 01821-3980.

AstroPower, Inc., (2002), "AstroPower Unveils New Rooftop-Integrated Solar Electric Power Systems", Nov. 12, (301) 366-0400 xt 2025.

Bazilian, M. D., Leenders, F., Van der Ree B. G. C. and Pras, D., (2001) "Photovoltaic co-generaton in the built environment", *Solar Energy*, Vol. 71(1), pp. 57–69.

Clearwater Australia Pty Ltd., 47 Myrtle Street, Glen Waverley, Victoria, Australia 3150, Voice: (03) 9561-6577, Fax: (03) 9561-6599. www. clearwater.com.au. A US distributor is Zodiac Pool Care, Inc., 5028 S. Ash Ave., Suite 108, Tempe, AZ 85282, Voice: (800) 937-7873. www.zodiacpoolcare.com

ClimateMaster, 7300 S. W. 44th St., Oklahoma City, Oklahoma, 73129, Phone: (405) 745-6000.

Davis Instruments, 3465 Diablo Avenue, Hayward, CA 94545-2778, Voice: (510) 732-9229 (in USA and Canada), (510) 732-7814 (outside USA or Canada), Fax: (510) 670-0589. www.davisnet.com

Deffeyes, Kenneth S., (2001), "*Hubberts's Peak: The Impending World Oil Shortage*," Princeton University Press, 208 pp.

Diablo Solar Services, Inc., 5021 Blum Road #2B, Martinez, CA 94553-9906, (925) 313-0600. www.diablosolar.com

Duffie, John A. and William A. Beckman., (1974), "*Solar Energy Thermal Processes*," John Wiley & Sons, NY, 386 pp.

Duffie, John A. and William A. Beckman., (1991), "*Solar Engineering of Thermal Processes*," John Wiley & Sons, NY, 919 pp.

EUREC Agency, (1997), "*The Future for Renewable Energy: Prospects and Directions*," James & James, London, 209 pp.

EUREC Agency, (2002), "*The Future for Renewable Energy: Prospects and Directions*," James & James, London, 250 pp.

FAFCO, Inc., 435 Otterson Drive, Chico, CA 95928-8207, Voice: (530) 332-2100, Fax (530) 332-2109. www.fafco.com

Fuel Cell Store at www.fuelcellstore.com. Located in Boulder, CO.

Galloway, T. R. and Joe Waidl., (2003) "Why Waste-to-Energy should be in any Country's Renewables Portfolio Standard," REFocus, International Renewable Energy Magazine, International Solar Energy Society. March/ April, pp. 30–31. Complete paper: Galloway, T. R. "Why Waste-to-Energy should be in any Country's Renewable Energy Portfolio," Energy Pulse Weekly: April 10. http://www.energypulse.net/centers/author.cfm?at_id=225

Galloway, T. R. and Ken Miller., (1996) "Demonstration of Residential Solar-Assisted Heat Pump System – Using Ground Coils, Radiant Floors, and Pool," Solar '96 Conference, July, American Solar Energy Society Annual Proceedings.

Galloway, T. R. and Gary Gerber., (1995) "Demonstration of Residential Solar-Assisted Heat Pump System – Using Ground Coils, Radiant Floors, and Pool," Solar '95 Conference, Minneapolis, MN, July 15–20, American Solar Energy Society Annual Proceedings. pp. 330–335.

Galloway, T. R., (1984) "A Solar Micro-Utility System for Buildings", 19th Intersociety Energy Conversion Engineering Conference, August 19–24, San Francisco, CA, pp. 168–1643.

Galloway, T. R., (1984) "New Opportunities and Challenges in Production of Methanol Fuels", 19th Intersociety Energy Conversion Engineering Conference, August 19–24, San Francisco, CA, pp. 648–653.

Galloway, T. R., (1983) "New Developments in Energy Recovery with Organic Rankine Bottoming Cycles", 18th Intersociety Energy Conversion Engineering Conference, August 21–26, Orlando, FL, pp. 662–667.

Galloway, T. R., (1981) "Solar assisted heat pump and swimming pool synergy for domestic heating", J. Solar Energy Engineering, 103, 105–112.

Galloway, T. R., (1980) "Solar Assisted Heat Pump Swimming Pool Synergistics for Domestic Heating," 2nd Annual Systems Simulation and Economics Analysis Conference, January 23–25, San Diego, CA and AIChE Meeting, Portland, OR, August 10–13, Lawrence Livermore National Lab. Rept. 83458 (1979).

Galloway, T. R., (1979) "Predicting Solar Energy Fluxes in Polluted Urban Areas", 14th Intersociety Energy Conversion Engineering Conference, August 5–10, Boston, MA, pp. 32–38.

Galloway, T. R., (1979) "Solar Energy Design Methods in Polluted Urban Areas", Hemisphere Press, in press.

Galloway, T. R., (1979) "Solar Energy Less Than Predicted", Chemical and Engineering News, 18 pp., August 13.

Galloway, T. R., (1979) "To Fix the Flux", Science News, 143 pp., August 25.

Galloway, T. R., (1979) "Available Solar Energy", Industrial Research/Development, 29 pp., September.

Galloway, T. R., (1979) "Solar Energy Design Methods for Polluted Urban Areas", Lawrence Berkeley Laboratory, Energy and Environmental Seminar, November 6.

Galloway, T. R., (1980) "Solar Assisted Heat Pump Swimming Pool Synergistics for Domestic Heating", 2nd Annual Systems Simulation and Economics Analysis Conference, January 23–25, San Diego, CA and AIChE Meeting, Portland, OR, August 10–13, Lawrence Livermore National Lab. Rept. 83458.

Galloway, T. R., (1978) "Paraffin Wax Heat-Storage for Solar Heated Homes", 13th Intersociety Energy Conversion Engineering Conference, August 20–25, San Diego, CA, pp. 963–969.

Galloway, T. R. and Porch, W. M., (1978) "Astronomical Opportunities", Chemistry 51, (1), 5–6.

Galloway, T. R., (1977) "Space Heating and Swimming Pool Heat", Energy Today, Vol. 1, September 13.

Galloway, T. R. and S. T. Massie., (1977) "Long Path Optical Monitoring", Lawrence Livermore Laboratory Rept. UCRL-78724.

Galloway, T. R. and S. T. Massie., (1977) "Optical Extinction as a Diagnostic Tool for Air Pollution", Lawrence Livermore Laboratory Rept. UCRL-78850.

Galloway, T. R., (1977) "A Plastic Solar Panel, Heat Storage, Baseboard Heating System for Both Swimming Pool and Home", 12th Intersociety Energy Conversion Engineering Conference, August 23–September 2, Washington, DC, pp. 1263–1268.

Galloway, T. R., (1975) "Optical Probe Monitoring of Air Pollution Particulates", Proceedings of the 2nd National Conference on Complete Water Reuse, May 18, Chicago, IL, pp. 324–330.

Geothermal Heat Pump Association, Oklahoma City, Oklahoma, USA.

Hamer, Glenn., (2003) "Seeing Green Elephants," *Solar Today*, May/June, pp. 28–29.

HelioDyne, Inc., 4910 Seaport Ave., Richmond, California 94804, Phone: (510) 237-9614. www.heliodyne.com

Hoffmann, Peter., (2001) "*Tomorrow's Energy: Hydrogen, Fuel Cells, and the Prospects for a Cleaner Planet*," The MIT Press, 289 pp.

Home Controls, Inc., 7626 Miramar Road, Suite 3300, San Diego, CA 92126. www.homecontrols.com

Invensys Energy Solutions, Building Systems – Americas, 1354 Clifford Ave Loves Park, IL 61111, and P.O. Box 2940, Loves Park, IL 61132–2940. www.ies.invensys.com

Intellergy Corporation, Private communication, June 2001.

Jade Mountain Catalog, (2002) Vol. XV (1), January.

James & James, "Meteonorm 2000, Version 4.0," science publishers, 8–12 Camden High St. London NW1 0JH, UK. www.jxj.com

Johnson, Jeff., (2003) "Another Gas Crisis," *Chem & Eng News*, Vol. 81(12), March 24.

Kreith, Frank and Jan F. Kreider., (1978), "*Principles of Solar Engineering*," Hemisphere Pub. Corp., NY, 778 pp.

Meinel, Aden B. and Marjorie P. Meinel., (1979), "Applied Solar Energy – An Introduction," 651 pp.

Nold, Edward, Nold Residential Design, 1934 Tiffin Road, Oakland, CA, (510) 531-1184. Design completed in 1995.

Powerlight Co., (2003) Berkeley, CA, (510) 540-0550 January 14. www.powerlight.com

Regency Industries Ltd., (1995) 7830 Vantage Way, Delta, B.C., Canada V4G 1A7.

Rifkin, Jeremy., (2002), "*The Hydrogen Economy*" Penguin Putnam, Inc., NY, 294 pp.

Sandnes, B. and John Rekstad., (2002) "A photovoltaic/thermal (PV/T) collector with a polymer absorber plate experimental study and analytical model, *Solar Energy*, Vol. 72(1), pp. 63–73.

Sanyo, Osaka, Japan, (2002) "Sanyo to Ramp up Solar Photovoltaic Market Position in Europe," www.solar buzz.com/News/NewsASCO20.htm, December 24.

Siebe Environmental Controls, 1354 Clifford Ave Loves Park, IL 61111, and P.O. Box 2940, Loves Park, IL 61132–2940. www.ies.invensys.com

Solar Energy Research Institute, (1988), "*Engineering Principles and Concepts for Active Solar Systems*," Hemisphere Pub. Corp., NY, 295 pp.

Sun Light & Power Co., 1035 Folger Avenue, Berkeley, CA 94710, Voice: (510) 845-2997, Fax: (510) 845-1133. www.sunlightandpower.com

Thermal Energy Systems, Inc., (1992) 805 West Fifth Street, Lansdale, PA 19446, Voice: (215) 361-1700, Fax: (215) 361-1845. Heat pump installation and operations manuals, March.

Williams, J. Richard., (1974), "*Solar Energy – Technology and Applications*," Ann Arbor Science, MI, 131 pp.

Yamas Controls, One South Linden Avenue, Suite 1, South San Francisco, CA 94080, Voice: (650) 616-7400, Fax: (650) 616-7409. www.Yamas.com

List of useful websites

AstroPower, Inc.	www.astropower.com
Alternative Energy Institute	www.altenergy.org
American Council for Energy Efficient Economy	www.aceee.org
American Council for Renewaable Energy	www.americanrenewables.org
American Solar Energy Society	www.ases.org
American Wind Energy Association	www.awea.org
Asian Alternative Energy Program	www.worldbank.org/astae/
British Wind Energy Association	www.bwea.com
California Energy Commission, State of California	www.energy.ca.gov
Canadian Wind Energy Association	www.canwea.ca
Clearwater Australia Pty Ltd.	www.clearwater.com.au.
Danish Wind Energy Association	www.worldbank.org/astae/
Davis Instruments	www.davisnet.com.
Daystar, Inc.	www.zianet.com/daystar
Diablo Solar Services, Inc.	www.diablosolar.com
Energy Council of Canada	www.energy.ca
Energy Efficiency and Renewable Energy Office of US DOE	www.eren.doe.gov
Energy Efficiency Consumers Guide	www.energyguide.com
Energy Efficiency Standards of US DOE	www.energystar.gov
Energy Ideas Trade Group	www.energyideas.org
Energy Industry Online Services	www.energyonline.com
Energy Pulse news site	www.energypulse.net
European Commission, Directorate on Energy and Transport	www.europa.eu.int/comm/dgs/energy_transport/index_en.html
European Renewable Energy	www.eurorex.com
European Wind Energy Association	www.ewea.org
FAFCO, Inc.	www.fafco.com
Fraunhofer Institute of Solar Energy Systems	www.ise.fhg.de
Fuel Cell Energy Corp.	www.fce.com
Fuel Cell Store	www.fuelcellstore.com
Fuel Cell Today International Industry news	www.fuelcelltoday.com
German Wind Energy Association	www.wind-energie.de

HelioDyne, Inc.	www.heliodyne.com
Home Controls, Inc.	www.homecontrols.com
Hydrogen Energy Center	www.h2eco.org
IEA Heat Pump Center	www.heatpumpcentre.org
Intellergy Corporation	www.intellergy.com
International Association for Hydrogen Energy	www.iahe.org
International Atomic Energy Agency	www.iaea.or.at
International Energy Agency	www.iea.org
International Solar Energy Society	www.ises.org
Invensys Energy Solutions, Building Systems – Americas	www.ies.invensys.com
Irish Sustainable Energy, National Agency	www.irish-energy.ie
Italian Energy and Environment Agency	www.enea.it
Jade Mountain Catalog	www.jademountain.com
James & James	www.jxj.com
Kipp & Zonen (USA) Inc.	www.kippzonen.com
Leadership in Energy and Enviromental Design – Building Rating	www.usgbc.org/LEED/index.asp
Levitron	www.Levitron.com
National Renewable Energy Laboroatory of US. DOE	www.nrel.gov
National Energy Foundation, UK	www.natenergy.org.uk
Ovonic/UniSolar	www.ovonic.com/unisolar.htm
PlugPower, a partnership with General Electric	www.plugpower.com
Powerlight Co.	www.powerlight.com
Proton Energy Systems	www.protonenergy.com
Residential Energy Efficiency Data Base, Canada	www.its-canada.com/reed
Rocky Mountain Institute	www.rmi.org
Sanyo, Osaka, Japan	www.solar buzz.com
Shatz Energy Research Center	www.humboldt.edu/~serc/index.shtml
Shell Energy Services for Home or Business	www.shellenergy.com
Sierra Club Energy Committee	www.sierraclub.org/energy/
Solar Energy Indusries Association	www.seia.org
Stuart Energy	www.stuartenergy.com
Sun Light & Power Co.	www.sunlightandpower.com
Sustainable Energy Coalition	www.sustainableenergy.org
US Congress House Committee on Energy and Commerce	www.energycommerce.house.gov
US Department of Energy	www.energy.gov
US DOE Building Energy Codes	www.energycodes.gov
US DOE Office of Energy Efficiency Guide to Consumers	www.eren.doe.gov/consumerinfo/energy_savers/
US DOE Photovoltaics Information Page	www.eere.energy.gov/pv/
US Energy Information Agency	www.eia.doe.gov
US EPA, Energy Star energy efficiency standards	www.epa.gov/energystar

US Executive Branch, National Energy Policy	www.whitehouse.gov/energy
US Federal Statistics on Energy Use	www.fedstats.gov/programs/energy.html
US Senate Committee on Energy & Natural Resources	www.senate.gov/~energy
UK Trust on Saving Energy	www.saveenergy.co.uk
UniSolar	www.unisolar.com
US DOE National Energy Technology Laboratory	www.netl.doe.gov
Valentin Energy Software	www.valentin.de
Wind Energy Resource Atlas for the US	www.rredc.nrel.gov/wind/pubs/atlas/
World Bank Energy Programs	www.worldbank.org/energy/
World Energy Council	www.worldenergy.org/wec-geis/
World Energy Efficiency Association	www.weea.org
World Energy News	www.worldenergynews.com
Yamas Controls	www.Yamas.com

Abbreviations

AF   Attic Fan
AV   Automatic Valve
BIPV   Building Integrated PV
COP   Coefficient Of Performance
CT   Current Toroid
DHW   Domestic Hot Water
EER   Energy Efficiency Ratio
EUREC   European Union Renewable Energy Council
FWD   Fan with Damper
GHPA   Geothermal Heat Pump Association
GW   GigaWatts = 1000 MegaWatts
HIT   Hetero-Junction with Intrinsic Thin-Layer Technology
HP   Heat Pump
HVAC   Heating, Ventilation, and Air Conditioning
HX   Heat Exchanger
MBR   Master Bedroom
MSW   Municipal Solid Waste
ORP   Oxidation Reduction Potential
PDA   Personal Digital Assistant
PEM   Polymer Membrane
PF   Paddle Fan
PM   Preventative Maintenance
PV   Photovoltaic
PVT   PV and Thermal Collector
RH   Radiant Heat
TIC   Temperature-Indicating Controllers
TOU   Time-Of-Use
UPS   Uninterruptible Power Supply

Glossary

Active heating   building heating systems that require pumps or fans for distributing heat to other locations in a building.

Adaptive controls   are those controls that get better and more efficient at automatically operating the solar house through "learning" what strategy works best.

Air mass   is the thickness of air through which the sunlight has to pass to arrive at a ground-level surface. Straight overhead (called zenith) the air mass is defined as unity and the air mass goes up directly with the secant of the angle away from the zenith. (Note: the secant is the reciprocal of the cosine.)

Central energy plants   centrally located steam or electric power plants that distribute their energy within a radius around the plant. Generally very large scale to achieve good economies.

Coefficient of performance   a heat pump is like using electric power to heat the floors, except that it is three or four times more efficient than using electric resistive heat. This big improvement factor over resistive heat is called the coefficient of performance (COP).

Coolth   is the opposite of heat being stored. It is the amount of cooling capacity being stored in a tank for space cooling.

Current sensor   or current toroid (CT), that consists of a small, inexpensive coil placed around a wire running between the energy source and the energy consuming device.

Decentralized energy plants   are small and local, supplying their energy products to the local area or locally at a building.

Electrolyzers   an electrical device which takes DC power and breaks down water to make hydrogen gas at the anode and oxygen gas at the cathode.

Geothermal heat pump   operates with one coil buried deep in the ground and the other one in the radiant floors. So the Freon® dumps its heat into a heat exchanger called "sink" which heats the glycol that runs through and heats the radiant floors. The other side of the heat pump has a heat exchanger called "source" which has ground temperature glycol circulating through it. So in this way heat from the ground is amplified by the heat pump and used to heat the radiant floor.

Ground-source heat pump   see geothermal heat pump.

Gypcrete   a special type of high thermal conductivity concrete used for radiantly heated floors to encase the radiant coils.

Heat convection   is when air carries heat away from a warm surface.

Heat transfer coefficient   is a measure of how well the heat from a solid surface is transferred to the adjacent air. A number over 60 Btu/hr-ft^2-°F (or 6 kW-m^2-°C) is very high as a result of moving air across the surface and around 1 Btu/hr-ft^2-°F (or 0.1 kW/m^2-°C) is very low when the surrounding air is stagnant.

Heating degree days   are the number of degrees the living space needs to be heated above 24°C (65°F) times the number of days heat is needed.

Insolation   the solar flux falling on a surface, measured in W/m^2.

Neural networks   a scheme that "learns" much like the human brain by making connections and memorizing through the association of facts or actions.

Nocturnal (free) cooling   bringing in cool air low in the building at night and exhausting the hotter air at the highest point to achieve cooling of the building.

Optimization of the control system   uses an objective function or objective measure that is used to decide if the control system change is better or worse.

Passive heat   heat that is obtained from the sunlight illuminating portions of a building that are designed to provide comfortable living conditions. No pumps or fans are generally used; this heat depends on natural convection circulation.

Photovoltaics (PV)   collector plates made of silicon and/or mixtures of rare earth metals that produce electricity when illuminated by solar light.

Pyranometer   is an optical instrumentation device that detects the solar heat flux falling onto a surface. The wavelength sensitivity is such that it provides an excellent measure of the solar energy falling on solar thermal collectors to check their performance efficiency.

Radiation   is the transfer of heat from a hot surface usually infrared radiation, thus heating the air or nearby surfaces.

Renewable energy (Renewables)   energy that is generated or extracted from natural sources that do not deplete resources of the earth; energy which is sustainably produced.

Reynolds number   is a dimensionless group used in fluid mechanics to measure the relative inertial forces of the flow divided by the viscous forces: density • velocity • tube diameter/absolute viscosity.

Solarium   is a sunroom with a large expanse of glass roof and walls that accepts sun and heats the space inside. Can also be a solar greenhouse for plants.

Stagnation   where the pumps, piping, or controls have failed and there is no flow through the collectors on a hot solar day and the solar collector temperature becomes unacceptably high.

Steam reforming   a chemical process wherein hydrocarbons (such as methane, or waste) are reacted at high temperature with steam to produce hydrogen gas, or syngas.

Syngas   synthetic gas consisting roughly, by volume, of 50% hydrogen, 25% carbon monoxide, 10% steam, 8% carbon dioxide, 6% methane, 1% light hydrocarbons, and other trace heavier organics.

Thermal conductivity   the ability to conduct heat from one location to another adjacent location when the two locations are at a different temperatures. A high number would be for concrete and a low number would be for insulation or air.

Thermal mass   a large mass object or wall where heat is stored by raising the temperature of this mass above the ambient air temperature.

Water source heat pumps   see geothermal heat pump.

Wheel   to move electric power over utility transmission wires from a location of generation to a location of consumption.

X-10®   power line carrier devices that will turn on lights, outlets, appliances, etc., and detect that they have turned on and send a confirming signal back to the local switch. Trademark of the Powerline Corporation.

Appendix

Figure A.1   Foundation concrete pour and start of framing.

Figure A.2   Architect Ed Nold (left) and general contractor Gary Gerber (right) standing on the start of the second floor on the bridge between the main living/kitchen/dining section to the second floor bedrooms.

Figure A.3   Assembled second floor walls ready to tilt up.

Figure A.4   Second floor walls nearing completion after tilt up.

Figure A.5   Roof framing on second floor complete and preparing for the long rafters for the solar roof over living/kitchen/dining section.

Figure A.6   Inside view of living/kitchen/dining section ready to install long rafters for solar roof.

Figure A.7   Solar roof rafters in place preparing for the topping of large insulating R-control foam panels.

Figure A.8   Completion of the solar roof construction by placement of the R-control panels over the long roof rafters to produce the interior exposed beam vaulted ceiling.

Index

Architectural Press

An imprint of Elsevier
www.architecturalpress.com

Visit **www.architecturalpress.com**

Our regularly updated website includes:

- News on our latest books
- Special offers, discounts and freebies
- Free downloadable sample chapters from our newest titles
- Links to companion websites giving you extra information on our books
- Author biographies and information
- Links to useful websites and extensive directories of relevant organisations and publications
- A search engine and a secure online ordering system for the entire catalogue of **Architectural Press** books

You can also get **free membership** of our **eNews** service by visiting our website to register. Once you are a member, you will receive a monthly email bulletin which gives you:

- Exclusive author articles
- The chance to enter prize draws for free books
- Access to offers and discounts exclusive to **eNews** members
- News of our latest books sent direct to your desktop

If you would like any other information about **www.architecturalpress.com** or our **eNews** service please contact:

Rachel Lace, Product Manager
Email: r.lace@elsevier.com
Tel: +44(0)1865 314594
Fax: +44(0)1865 314572
Address: Architectural Press, Linacre House, Jordan Hill, Oxford, OX28 DP, UK